Human Rights in Business

The capacity to abuse, or in general affect the enjoyment of human, labour and environmental rights has risen with the increased social and economic power that multinational companies wield in the global economy. At the same time, it appears that it is difficult to regulate the activities of multinational companies in such a way that they conform to international human, labour and environmental rights standards. This has partially to do with the organization of companies into groups of separate legal persons, incorporated in different states, as well as with the complexity of the corporate supply chain. Absent a business and human rights treaty, a more coherent legal and policy approach is required.

Faced with the challenge of how to effectively access the right to remedy in the European Union for human rights abuses committed by EU companies in non-EU states, a diverse research consortium of academic and legal institutions was formed. The consortium, coordinated by the Globernance Institute for Democratic Governance, became the recipient of a 2013 Civil Justice Action Grant from the European Commission Directorate General for Justice. A mandate was thus issued for research, training and dissemination so as to bring visibility to the challenge posed and moreover, to provide some solutions for the removal of barriers to judicial and non-judicial remedy for victims of business-related human rights abuses in non-EU states. The project commenced in September 2014 and over the course of two years the consortium conducted research along four specific lines in parallel with various training sessions across EU Member States.

The research conducted focused primarily on judicial remedies, both jurisdictional barriers and applicable law barriers; non-judicial remedies, both to company-based grievance. The results of this research endeavour make up the content of this report whose aim is to provide a scholarly foundation for policy proposals by identifying specific challenges relevant to access to justice in the European Union and to provide recommendations on how to remove legal and practical barriers so as to provide access to remedy for victims of business-related human rights abuses in non-EU states.

Juan José Álvarez Rubio is Professor of Private International Law at the University of the Basque Country (UPV/EHU), Spain and Secretary of the Globernance Institute for Democratic Governance.

Katerina Yiannibas is an Assistant Professor of Public and Private International Law at Deusto University, Spain and a researcher at the Globernance Institute for Democratic Governance.

HUMAN RIGHTS IN BUSINESS CO-BENEFICIARY INSTITUTIONS

UNIVERSITY OF NAVARRA
FRANK BOLD SOCIETY
UNIVERSITY OF CASTILLA-LA MANCHA
UNIVERSITY OF JAUME I
ROVIRA I VIRGILI UNIVERSITY
PROFESSOR CEES VAN DAM CONSULTANCY LTD.
LUDWIG BOLTZMANN INSTITUTE OF HUMAN RIGHTS
TILBURG UNIVERSITY
UTRECHT UNIVERSITY
LEIDEN UNIVERSITY
PUBLIC UNIVERSITY OF NAVARRA
CUATRECASAS, GONÇALVES PEREIRA
UNIVERSITY OF RIJEKA
GLOBERNANCE INSTITUTE FOR DEMOCRATIC GOVERNANCE

This project is co-funded by the European Union

GLOBERNANCE

GOBERNANTZA DEMOKRATIKOAREN INSTITUTUA
INSTITUTO DE GOBERNANZA DEMOCRÁTICA

Disclaimer: This publication has been produced with the financial support of the Civil Justice Programme of the European Union. The contents of this publication are the sole responsibility of the authors and can in no way be taken to reflect the views of the European Commission.

Human Rights in Business

Removal of Barriers to Access to Justice in the European Union

Edited by
Juan José Álvarez Rubio
and Katerina Yiannibas

Routledge
Taylor & Francis Group
LONDON AND NEW YORK

First published 2017
by Routledge

2 Park Square, Milton Park, Abingdon, Oxfordshire OX14 4RN
711 Third Avenue, New York, NY 10017

Routledge is an imprint of the Taylor & Francis Group, an informa business

First issued in paperback 2018

British Library Cataloguing-in-Publication Data
A catalogue record for this book is available from the British Library

Library of Congress Cataloging-in-Publication Data
Names: Rubio, Juan José Álvarez, editor. | Yiannibas, Katerina, editor.
Title: Human rights in business : removal of barriers to access to justice in the European Union / edited by Juan José Álvarez Rubio and Katerina Yiannibas.
Description: Abingdon, Oxon ; New York, NY : Routledge, 2017. | Includes bibliographical references and index.
Identifiers: LCCN 2016042618 | ISBN 9781138284180 (hbk) | ISBN 9781315269467 (ebk)
Subjects: LCSH: Liability for human rights violations—European Union countries. | Tort liability of corporation—European Union countries.
Classification: LCC KJE1635 .H86 2017 | DDC 344.2401—dc23
LC record available at https://lccn.loc.gov/2016042618

ISBN: 978-1-138-28418-0 (hbk)
ISBN: 978-0-367-02516-8 (pbk)

Typeset in Galliard
by Apex CoVantage, LLC

Contents

Notes on contributors

Daniel Augenstein works as Associate Professor in the Department of European and International Public Law at Tilburg Law School.

Sandrine Brachotte is a Legal Consultant at Frank Bold Society.

L.F.H. (Liesbeth) Enneking is an Assistant Professor at UCALL, the Utrecht Centre for Accountability and Liability Law of Utrecht University.

Filip Gregor is Head of the Responsible Companies Section at Frank Bold Society.

Katharina Häusler worked as a researcher at the Ludwig Boltzmann Institute of Human Rights until August 2016.

Nicola Jägers holds the Chair International Human Rights Law at the Law School of Tilburg University in the Netherlands.

Karin Lukas is a senior researcher at the Ludwig Boltzmann Institute of Human Rights and member of the European Committee of Social Rights (Council of Europe).

Paige Morrow is Head of Brussels operations at Frank Bold Society.

Pablo Paisán Ruiz is a lawyer at Cuatrecasas, Gonçalves Pereira.

Julia Planitzer is a senior researcher at Ludwig Boltzmann Institute of Human Rights.

Lucas Roorda is a researcher at the Institute of International, Social and Economic Public Law at Utrecht University and member of the Utrecht Centre for Accountability and Liability Law (UCALL).

Juan José Álvarez Rubio is Professor of Private International Law at the University of the Basque Country (UPV/EHU), Spain and Secretary of the Globernance Institute for Democratic Governance.

Cees van Dam is Professor of International Business and Human Rights at the Rotterdam School of Management (Erasmus University), teaches as a Visiting Professor English and Comparative Tort Law at King's College London, and is Honorary Professor of European Private Law at Utrecht University and is part time Professor of European Tort Law at Maastricht University.

Katerina Yiannibas is an Assistant Professor of Public and Private International Law at Deusto University and a researcher at the Globernance Institute for Democratic Governance.

is Honorary Professor of European Private Law at Utrecht University and is part time Professor of European Tort Law at Maastricht University.

Katerina Yiannibas is an Assistant Professor of Public and Private International Law at Deusto University and a researcher at the Globernance Institute for Democratic Governance.

Notes on contributors

Daniel Augenstein works as Associate Professor in the Department of European and International Public Law at Tilburg Law School.

Sandrine Brachotte is a Legal Consultant at Frank Bold Society.

L.F.H. (Liesbeth) Enneking is an Assistant Professor at UCALL, the Utrecht Centre for Accountability and Liability Law of Utrecht University.

Filip Gregor is Head of the Responsible Companies Section at Frank Bold Society.

Katharina Häusler worked as a researcher at the Ludwig Boltzmann Institute of Human Rights until August 2016.

Nicola Jägers holds the Chair International Human Rights Law at the Law School of Tilburg University in the Netherlands.

Karin Lukas is a senior researcher at the Ludwig Boltzmann Institute of Human Rights and member of the European Committee of Social Rights (Council of Europe).

Paige Morrow is Head of Brussels operations at Frank Bold Society.

Pablo Paisán Ruiz is a lawyer at Cuatrecasas, Gonçalves Pereira.

Julia Planitzer is a senior researcher at Ludwig Boltzmann Institute of Human Rights.

Lucas Roorda is a researcher at the Institute of International, Social and Economic Public Law at Utrecht University and member of the Utrecht Centre for Accountability and Liability Law (UCALL).

Juan José Álvarez Rubio is Professor of Private International Law at the University of the Basque Country (UPV/EHU), Spain and Secretary of the Globernance Institute for Democratic Governance.

Cees van Dam is Professor of International Business and Human Rights at the Rotterdam School of Management (Erasmus University), teaches as a Visiting Professor English and Comparative Tort Law at King's College London, and

Acknowledgments

The research leading to this report has received funding from the European Commission's Civil Justice Programme under the Action Grant JUST/2013/JCIV/AG/4661. The research consortium, led by the Globernance Institute for Democratic Governance, is composed of a diverse set of legal scholars and practitioners from various EU Member States: Juan José Álvarez Rubio (Globernance Institute for Democratic Governance), Daniel Augenstein (Tilburg University), María Victoria Camarero Suárez (University of Jaume I), Antonio Cardesa-Salzmann (Rovira i Virgili University), A.G. Castermans (Leiden University), Liesbeth F.H. Enneking (Utrecht University), María Font Mas (Rovira i Virgili University), Filip Gregor (Frank Bold Society), Katharina Häusler (Ludwig Boltzmann Institute of Human Rights), José Luis Iriarte Ángel (Public University of Navarra), Nicola Jägers (Tilburg University), Ivana Kunda (University of Rijeka), Eduard Kunstek (University of Rijeka), Karin Lukas (Ludwig Boltzmann Institute of Human Rights), Daniel Iglesias Márquez (Rovira i Virgili University), Jordi Jaria Manzano (Rovira i Virgili University), José Antonio Moreno Molina (University of Castilla-La Mancha), Paige Morrow (Frank Bold Society), Alberto Muñoz Fernández (University of Navarra), Pablo Paisán Ruiz (Cuatrecasas Gonçalves Pereira SLP), Lorena Sales Pallarés (University of Castilla-La Mancha), Augustín Viguri Perea (University of Jaume I), Antoni Pigrau Solé (Rovira i Virgili University), Julia Planitzer (Ludwig Boltzmann Institute of Human Rights), Lucas Roorda (Utrecht University), María Álvarez Torné (University of Barcelona), Cees van Dam (Professor Cees van Dam Consultancy Ltd.), Katerina Yiannibas (Globernance Institute for Democratic Governance), and Francisco Javier Zamora Cabot (University of Jaume I). Particular recognition and appreciation is given to Nicolás Zambrana Tevár for bringing together the consortium.

The authors would like to thank the following individuals for their valuable inputs: Carmen Agoués Mendizabal (Spain), José Miguel Ayerza (Spain), Denis Bensaude (France), Robin Bouvier (France), Stéphane Brabant (France), David Chivers, QC (UK), Sandra Cossart (France), Brooks W. Daly (Netherlands), Ingrid Gubbay (UK), Patrick Harty (UK), Mariëtte van Huijstee (Netherlands), Charlotte Jacobs (Netherlands), Lise Johnson (US), Rasmus Kløcker Larsen (Sweden), Niki Koumadoraki (Austria), Nerea Magallón Elósegui (Spain), Yvon

Martinet (France), María Chiara Marullo (Spain), Robert McCorquodale (UK), Sarah McGrath (US), Vanesa Menendez (Spain), Krishnendu Mukherjee (UK), Telmo Olascoaga (Spain), Marta Requejo Isidro (Luxembourg), Cedric Ryngaert (Netherlands), Urs Rybi (Switzerland), Channa Samkalden (Netherlands), Anne Scheltema Beduin (Netherlands), John Sherman (US), Christopher Schuller (Germany), Gwynne Skinner (US). The authors would also like to thank the Austrian Federal Ministry of Labour, Social Affairs and Consumer Protection (BMASK), the Business Association of Gipuzkoa (Adegi), the Chamber of Labour Vienna, the European Capital of Culture San Sebastian 2016 Foundation, the European Coalition for Corporate Justice (ECCJ), the European Network of National Human Rights Institutions (ENNHRI), the Ministry of Foreign Affairs of the Netherlands, the MVO Platform, the San Telmo Museum, and the Centre for Research on Multinational Corporations (SOMO) for their contributions and support.

Introduction

Katerina Yiannibas and Lucas Roorda

On 24 April 2013, a factory collapsed in the Savar subdistrict of Bangladesh, killing more than 1,100 people and injuring more than 3,000. Three years later, the name of that factory is synonymous with irresponsible business practices: Rana Plaza. Following the disaster, many reports came out about the working conditions in the factory, overcrowding and the substandard construction of the factory itself. The criticism was not just confined to the Rana Plaza factory, but was directed at the whole of the Bangladeshi clothing industry and its buyers, many of which are company brands based in the European Union (EU). Garments from Rana Plaza were allegedly made for Spanish clothing giant Zara, Italian fashion house Benetton, and Irish retailer Primark.

However, it is not just European clothing companies that are accused of irresponsible behaviour.[1] Other examples include European resource extraction companies whose activities were connected to environmental damage in local communities, or that have worked together with authoritarian regimes to suppress protests against those environmental impacts. Yet other European companies have been accused of maintaining unsafe and unhealthy working environments in production facilities operated by their subsidiaries, or violating other labour rights.[2]

The capacity to abuse, or in general affect the enjoyment of human, labour and environmental rights, has risen with the increased social and economic power that multinational companies (MNCs) wield in the global economy. At the same time, it appears that it is difficult to regulate the activities of MNCs

1 The term 'company' is used here to denominate non-governmental, for-profit entities with legal personality that conduct commercial transactions. The word 'companies' appears to be more common in the European context, whereas American and Canadian authors tend to refer more to these entities as 'corporations'. As this report concerns the European Union, the authors have opted for the former, noting that for the purposes of this work the two terms can be regarded as synonyms.

2 See for a (non-exhaustive) list of judicial complaints on these issues against European companies, the website of the Business & Human Rights Resource Centre, https://business-humanrights.org/en/corporate-legal-accountability/case-profiles/country-where-lawsuit-filed/europe-central-asia.

in such a way that they conform to international human, labour and environmental rights standards. This has partially to do with the organization of companies into groups of separate legal persons, incorporated in different states, as well as with the complexity of the corporate supply chain.[3] Absent a business and human rights treaty, a more coherent legal and policy approach is required.

The debate regarding this policy approach is currently governed by the United Nations Guiding Principles on Business and Human Rights ('UN Guiding Principles' or UNGPs).[4] Unanimously endorsed by the UN Human Rights Council as an operationalization of the 2008 'Protect, Respect and Remedy' Framework, the UN Guiding Principles have sought to clarify the respective roles and responsibilities of states, businesses and those affected by business-related human rights abuses. The 2008 Framework and the Guiding Principles do so through a three-pillar structure: the state duty to protect against third-party human rights abuses, the corporate responsibility to respect human rights of those affected by their operations, and the right of victims to an effective remedy if human rights abuses do occur.

The UN Guiding Principles are but the start of the debate, laying down issues to be addressed and providing the terminology with which the debate can be conducted. The actual legal and policy developments have to come from states themselves, in pursuance of their obligations and responsibilities under human rights law. Nowhere is this emphasized more than under the First Pillar and General Principle 1, putting on states the obligation to 'protect against human rights abuse within their territory and/or jurisdiction by third parties, including business enterprises.' States are thus still the primary actors in securing an optimum respect for human rights in business activities.

The state duty to protect is complemented by the right of victims to an effective remedy. No matter how clear expectations are for companies to conduct their activities responsibly, no matter how well developed the legal regime governing those activities is, there will always be the need for a remedy for victims, when business operations adversely affect their human rights. Nevertheless, in the first five years after the adoption of the UN Guiding Principles, the third pillar and the right to remedy have received scarce attention. While some of the national action plans that have currently been published do acknowledge the relevance of the Third Pillar and the right to remedy, the attention paid to the Third Pillar in relation to the first two pillars is limited and very few concrete recommendations can yet be found.[5]

3 R. Mares, Limits of Supply Chain Responsibility: A Critical Analysis of Corporate Responsibility Instruments (2010) *Nordic Journal of International Law*, 79, No 2.

4 UN HRC, 'Guiding Principles on Business and Human Rights: Implementing the United Nations' "Protect, Respect and Remedy" Framework', A/HRC/17/31, 21 March 2011.

5 See for a general overview of the National Action Plans drafted thus far, UN OCHCR, State National Action Plans, available at http://www.ohchr.org/EN/Issues/Business/Pages/NationalActionPlans.aspx. Note that of those NAPs already written and published, all but Colombia and Norway are EU Member States, the latter of course having strong ties with the EU.

The right to remedy comprises a large spectrum of interrelated mechanisms, some explicitly addressed in the UN Guiding Principles, some more implicitly present. At the core are state-based, judicial remedies as recognized in General Principle 26, but non-judicial and non-state based mechanisms also play an additional part. Regarding judicial mechanisms, states have an obligation to remove 'legal, practical and other relevant barriers' to effective remedies. Such barriers may include lack of jurisdiction by the courts of a particular state, questions of which law is to be applied, absence of duties of care on the parent company, availability of legal funding and representation, and many others. Overcoming these barriers requires of states that they develop a clear view of which barriers are problematic in their own legal systems, and develop coherent policies as to how they will address those barriers.

The relevance of this question does not emanate solely from the UN Guiding Principles. Victims of business-related human rights abuses have increasingly been seeking remedies in the domestic legal systems of the parent companies related to a particular rights abuse. This movement has for a time mostly been present in the US, where the Alien Tort Statute (ATS)[6] has made it possible for plaintiffs coming from third states to file tort claims over violations of international human rights law by US as well as foreign companies in US federal courts. However, the US Supreme Court's recent decisions in *Kiobel v Royal Dutch Shell* (133 S.Ct. 1659 (2013)) regarding the extraterritorial reach of the ATS, and *Daimler AG v Bauman* (134 S. Ct. 746 (2014)) on the limits of personal jurisdiction in US courts, have made US courts less attractive for such claims. Already, more and more litigants find their way into European courts concerning human rights abuses connected to European companies, either through civil litigation, or as injured parties in criminal cases. With the ATS now less accessible to plaintiffs litigating against non-US companies, this can only be expected to increase.

These are the developments with which the EU is now confronted. As one of the early supporters of the UNGP project, the EU plays a 'leading role in the interrelation between business and human rights', recognizing the UNGPs as the 'authoritative policy framework'.[7] That policy framework permeates the EU's competences in several ways, as the business and human rights debate is present in many legal and policy areas. In the area of access to justice, however, the EU shares part of those competences with the Member States. Some are fully harmonized, such as the applicable law question under the Rome II Regulation; some are partially harmonized, such as civil jurisdiction under the Brussels I bis Regulation; and yet others are not harmonized at all, such as non-judicial remedies or the availability of legal aid. Any discussion on how the EU should

6 28 United States Code §1350.

7 Commission Staff Working Document on Implementing the UN Guiding Principles on Business and Human Rights – State of Play, Brussels, 15 July 2015, SWD (2015) 144 final. See also Council of the European Union Conclusions on Business and Human Rights, 20 June 2016, 10254/16.

deal with remedies for business-related human rights abuses must also take into account the diversity of competences and policy powers between the EU and the Member States on any particular issue.

The authors of this report acknowledge the work of several authors that have contributed to this discussion with analyses and recommendations, to which this report hopes to build upon in the specific context of the EU. Key to the debate on the right to remedy has been the 'Third Pillar: Access to Judicial Remedies for Human Rights Violations by Transnational Business' report by Professor Gwynne Skinner, Professor Robert McCorquodale, Professor Olivier De Schutter, and Andie Lambe for the International Corporate Accountability Roundtable (ICAR), CORE, and the European Coalition for Corporate Justice (ECCJ). Also key in the area of right to remedy has been the Report of the United Nations High Commissioner for Human Rights on 'Improving accountability and access to remedy for victims of business-related human rights abuse', A/HRC/32/19.

As regards recent work on business and human rights in the European context, two documents have been of specific relevance. First, the European Commission Staff Working Document on Implementing the UN Guiding Principles on Business and Human Rights – State of Play', an internal document describing the measures currently taken by the EU and possible gaps in implementing the UNGPs. Secondly, the Recommendation of the Committee of Ministers to Member States on human rights and business (CDDH-CORP (2015) R4, appendix II) drafted by the Council of Europe's drafting group on Human Rights and Business. While not specifically on the right to remedy, both of these documents have been informative with regards to the work that has already been done in the area of business and human rights responsibilities in Europe.

Discussing the right to remedy in the area of business and human rights is not just relevant for policy-makers and academics, but also for practitioners involved with business and human rights litigation. While plaintiffs have increasingly found their way into EU domestic courts to pursue their claims, indeed only a handful of these claims have led to a final verdict, as most have been settled at an early stage or dismissed before being argued on the merits.[8] Many issues are still left unclear for courts and litigants alike. Even taking into account the partial harmonization of European private international law, there is considerable diversity amongst EU Member States as to the rules pertaining to civil litigants in business and human rights cases. Familiarity with cases from one jurisdiction may not necessarily help claimants find their way in another. Thus, a more comprehensive guide for litigants on the obstacles they may face in

8 R. Meeran, 'Access to remedy: The United Kingdom experience of MNC tort litigation for human rights violations' in S. Deva and D. Bilchitz (eds.), *Human Rights Obligations of Business: Beyond the Corporate Responsibility to Respect*? Cambridge: Cambridge University Press, 2013.

bringing and arguing their case in various European courts is of great practical use.

Faced with the challenge of how to effectively access the right to remedy in the EU for human rights abuses committed by EU companies in non-EU states, a diverse research consortium of academic and legal institutions was formed.[9] The consortium, coordinated by the Globernance Institute for Democratic Governance, became the recipient of a 2013 Civil Justice Action Grant from the European Commission Directorate General for Justice. A mandate was thus issued for research, training and dissemination so as to bring visibility to the challenge posed and, moreover, to provide some solutions for the removal of barriers to judicial and non-judicial remedy for victims of business-related human rights abuses in non-EU states. The project commenced in September 2014 and over the course of two years the consortium conducted research along four specific lines in parallel with various training sessions across EU Member States. The research conducted focused primarily on judicial remedies, both jurisdictional barriers and applicable law barriers; non-judicial remedies, both company-based grievance mechanisms and international arbitration; and substantive law barriers concerning the corporate responsibility to respect human rights vis-à-vis a legal duty of care, with the goal of providing feasible legal recommendations for the EU and Member States.[10] At various research stages, external input was requested to engage stakeholders by way of questionnaires or peer review.

The results of this research endeavour make up the content of this report, the aim of which is to provide a scholarly foundation for policy proposals by identifying specific challenges relevant to access to justice in the EU, and to provide recommendations on how to remove legal and practical barriers so as to provide access to remedy for victims of business-related human rights abuses in non-EU states.

Chapters I and II analyse issues related to access to judicial remedies. Chapter I addresses the jurisdictional challenges that victims of human rights abuses committed by EU-based MNCs abroad face in seeking redress in EU Member State courts. The role of international human rights law in private litigation for human rights abuses by MNCs is analysed. The allocation of jurisdiction in transnational tort litigations against MNCs in the EU is discussed and compared with the US. Moreover, residual jurisdiction is addressed – the

9 The research consortium is composed of the University of Navarra, Frank Bold Society, University of Castilla-La Mancha, University of Jaume I, Rovira I Virgili University, Cees van Dam Consultancy Ltd., Ludwig Boltzmann Institute of Human Rights, Tilburg University, Utrecht University, Leiden University, Public University of Navarra, Cuatrecasas Gonçalves Pereira SLP, University of Rijeka, and coordinated by the Globernance Institute for Democratic Governance.

10 The research focused mainly on civil rather than criminal liability. The choice to focus on civil litigation was taken in light of the fact that criminal laws cannot always be applied against corporations in many European jurisdictions.

rules of jurisdiction governing third-state defendants. In conclusion, Chapter I offers some recommendations on how jurisdictional challenges can be addressed.

Chapter II addresses the issues concerning applicable law. It thus deals with the question of under what circumstances the national rules of tort law of the EU Member States would be applied in foreign direct liability cases brought before EU Member State courts against EU-based internationally operating companies in relation to the harmful impacts of their activities – or those of their subsidiaries or business partners – on people and the environment in non-EU host countries. In addition, Chapter II also addresses some of the main practical and procedural barriers that host country victims of corporate human rights or environmental abuse may encounter when seeking to get access to remedy before EU Member State courts.

Chapter III addresses the effectiveness of non-judicial remedies, in particular, company-based grievance mechanisms and international arbitration. Analysis is presented through detailed case studies on the company-based grievance mechanisms of Siemens and Statoil, as well as a case study on the potential of the arbitration mechanism conducted under the auspices of the Permanent Court of Arbitration (PCA). The effectiveness of each mechanism is evaluated based on criteria established by the UN Guiding Principles: legitimacy, accessibility, predictability, equitability, transparency, rights-compatibility, a source of continuous learning, and engagement and dialogue.

Chapter IV deals with the intersection of corporate responsibility to respect human rights and European tort law in the context of complex corporate structures and business relationships. More specifically, it considers the relationship between a company's duty of care and the same company's responsibility to address adverse human rights impacts linked to its operations, products or services by its business relationships. Chapter IV describes three options for legal reform to facilitate corporate responsibility to respect human rights: a disclosure obligation in civil law procedure with respect to the defendant-company's control over its business partner, a shift of the burden of proof to the defendant-company to prove that it did not exercise such control when available evidence show control prima facie, and a statutory duty for a company to identify, prevent and take action to cease human rights abuses by its business partners, analogous to the human rights due diligence outlined in the United Nations Guiding Principles on Business and Human Rights, connected with liability for the consequential damage.

Each chapter, each set of issues, is accompanied by a set of recommendations. It is our hope that the academic content of these pages translates into acts.

1 Judicial remedies

The issue of jurisdiction

Daniel Augenstein and Nicola Jägers

1.1 Overview

This chapter addresses jurisdictional challenges that third-country victims of human rights abuses committed by EU-based 'multinational' companies (MNCs) face in seeking redress in EU Member State courts. In general terms, private international law allocates jurisdiction to courts on the basis of a nexus to the forum state. In the EU, this general rule finds an expression in the requirement that the defendant of a civil action must be domiciled in one of the EU Member States. This creates difficulties in cases of private litigation for human rights abuses committed by MNCs where parts of these companies are domiciled outside the EU. While from an economic point of view, MNCs operate as globally integrated entities, they appear in law as a multitude of separate legal companies with different 'nationalities'. An important consequence of this legal sequestration is that victims of human rights abuses committed by EU-based MNCs outside the EU face significant obstacles in seeking redress in EU Member State courts, should they find no effective remedy in their home state. On the one hand, while EU Member State courts generally have jurisdiction over (parent) companies domiciled in the EU, it proves difficult to establish the liability of these companies in substantive law for human rights abuses committed by their subsidiaries and contractors in third countries. On the other hand, while third-country victims of human rights abuses often encounter difficulties in obtaining effective redress in their home countries, Member State courts will as a general rule decline jurisdiction in cases directly brought against these foreign subsidiaries and contractors in the EU.

In the second section, these challenges are addressed by way of examining the impact of the human right to access to justice and effective remedies on the allocation of jurisdiction in private international law. Against this background, the third section compares the allocation of jurisdiction under private international law in the European Union (Brussels I Regulation) and the United States. Particular reference is made to the US Alien Tort Claims Statute, until recently a preferred forum for victims seeking civil redress for human rights abuses committed by MNCs. The final section of the chapter analyses three avenues for establishing jurisdiction of EU Member State courts over human rights abuses committed by foreign companies in cases not covered by the Brussels I Regulation ('residual jurisdiction').

1.2 Impact of international human rights law on jurisdiction in private international law

1.2.1 Introduction

International human rights law can play an important role in private litigation for human rights abuses by MNCs. International human rights treaties impose obligations on states to prevent and redress corporate human rights abuses within their (human rights) jurisdiction. As public institutions of the state, civil courts adjudicating disputes between private parties are directly bound by these human rights obligations. This includes obligations to ensure victims' access to justice and to effective civil remedies. The important role of the state in ensuring effective civil remedies for victims of corporate human rights abuses has been recognized in the United Nations Guiding Principles on Business and Human Rights (UNGPs):

> States should take appropriate steps to ensure the effectiveness of domestic judicial mechanisms when addressing business-related human rights abuses, including considering ways to reduce legal, practical and other relevant barriers that could lead to a denial of access to remedy.[1]

In particular, states should 'ensure that they do not erect barriers to prevent legitimate cases from being brought before the courts in situations where judicial recourse is an essential part of accessing remedy or alternative sources of remedy are unavailable'. This also applies to transnational or cross-border litigations where 'claimants face a denial of justice in a host State and cannot access home State courts regardless of the merits of the claim'.[2]

Against this background, the present section focuses on two issues: the obligations of EU Member States to protect human rights in private litigations against MNCs and the impact of these obligations on the allocation of jurisdiction in private international law. Substantively, the primary focus is on the European Convention on Human Rights (ECHR). All Member States of the EU are also contracting parties to the ECHR. While, until accession, the EU is not directly bound by the ECHR, the latter plays an important role in the interpretation of EU law including the EU's own human rights instrument, the EU Charter of Fundamental Rights.

1 UN HRC, *Guiding Principles on Business and Human Rights: Implementing the United Nations 'Protect, Respect and Remedy' Framework*, A/HRC/17/31 (21 March 2011), 26.
2 *Ibid.*

1.2.2 Human rights in private litigation

The relationship between human rights and private litigation can be approached from two different perspectives. The first perspective, germane to private lawyers, asks whether and to what extent civil litigation can be used to vindicate values and interests protected by human rights, such as physical integrity, privacy, or individual property. Here, the relationship between corporate perpetrators and victims of human rights abuses is regulated by private law, and the principal aim of litigation is the award of pecuniary damages. The second perspective, germane to public lawyers, asks what obligations international human rights law imposes on states to protect human rights in the relationship between private actors. Here, the emphasis is on state duties to prevent and redress corporate human rights abuses through domestic legislation, adjudication, and the proper administration of justice.

It is widely accepted that international human rights treaties impose (positive) obligations on states to protect human rights in the relationship between private actors, including obligations to ensure access to justice and effective civil remedies for human rights abuses committed by ('multinational') corporations. According to the UN Human Rights Committee, for example, a state's human rights obligations 'will only be fully discharged if individuals are protected by the state, not just against abuses of Covenant rights by its agents, but also against acts committed by private persons or entities that would impair the enjoyment of Covenant rights'. Inversely, a state may violate its international human rights obligations if it fails 'to take appropriate measures or to exercise due diligence to prevent, punish or redress the harm caused by such acts by private persons or entities'.[3] The ECHR imposes some obligations on EU Member States to secure in their domestic law the individual's legal status, rights, and privileges necessary for an effective enjoyment of their human rights. These obligations also require states to ensure human rights protection in the relationship between companies and individuals, for example, in the employment context.

In *Wilson*, the applicants petitioned the European Court of Human Rights (ECtHR) on grounds of violations of Article 10 (freedom of expression) and Article 11 (freedom of assembly) because their employer companies had offered them financial incentives to renounce their rights to collective bargaining. The House of Lords (now the UK Supreme Court) did not find the actions of the companies in violation of domestic law. The ECtHR, by contrast, ruled that the state must uphold the rights of workers to use trade unions to represent them in negotiations with employers:

> The Court observes at the outset that although the essential object of Article 11 is to protect the individual against arbitrary interference by public authorities with the exercise of the rights protected, there may in addition

3 HRC, General Comment No. 31, *Nature of the General Legal Obligation Imposed on States Parties to the Covenant*, CCPR/C/21/Rev.1/Add.13 (26 May 2004) para. 8.

> be positive obligations to secure the effective enjoyment of these rights. In the present case, the matters about which the applicants complain . . . did not involve direct intervention by the State. The responsibility of the United Kingdom would, however, be engaged if these matters resulted from a failure on its part to secure to the applicants under domestic law the rights set forth in Article 11 of the Convention . . . [The Court] considers that, by permitting employers to use financial incentives to induce employees to surrender important union rights, the respondent State has failed in its positive obligation to secure the enjoyment of the rights under Article 11 of the Convention. This failure amounted to a violation of Article 11, as regards both the applicant trade unions and the individual applicants.[4]

The ECHR also imposes obligations on EU Member States concerning the judicial process, law enforcement, and the proper administration of justice. The court's case law suggests that states are duty-bound to investigate, punish and redress corporate human rights abuses when they occur. Where the legislative framework itself is deficient, states can be obliged to introduce new, or amend existing, legislation. Domestic courts are under an obligation to ensure access to justice and effective remedies when adjudicating private disputes between corporate perpetrators and victims of human rights abuses. The right to an effective remedy has both a procedural and a substantive dimension. A victim must have practical and meaningful access to a procedure that is capable of ending and repairing the effects of the violation. Once the violation is established, the victim must receive a relief sufficient to repair the harm.

In *Steel and Morris*, the ECtHR had to consider fair trial rights under Article 6 ECHR in defamation proceedings brought by an MNC against NGO campaigners in the UK. In its judgment, the court recalled that

> [t]he Convention is intended to guarantee practical and effective rights. This is particularly so of the right of access to a court in view of the prominent place held in a democratic society by the right to a fair trial. It is central to the concept of fair trial, in civil as in criminal proceedings, that a litigant is not denied the opportunity to present his or her case effectively before the court and that he or she is able to enjoy equality of arms with the opposing side.[5]

Applying these principles to the case at hand, the ECtHR concluded that the applicants were denied the possibility to effective legal representation before the domestic court:

> The disparity between the respective levels of legal assistance enjoyed by the applicants and [the company] was of such a degree that it could not

4 ECtHR *Wilson, National Union of Journalists and Others v The United Kingdom* (Judgment of 02 July 2002) paras 41, 48.

5 ECtHR *Steel and Morris v The United Kingdom* (Judgment of 15 February 2005) para. 59.

> have failed, in this exceptionally demanding case, to have given rise to unfairness . . . The lack of procedural fairness and equality therefore gave rise to a breach of Article 10 in the present case.[6]

1.2.3 International human rights law and jurisdiction in private international law

There are several ways in which private international law can accommodate concerns for human rights protection, including through the recognition of special grounds of jurisdiction such as *forum necessitatis*. The latter, which is discussed in more detail in section 1.4, raises a more general question as concerns the relationship between jurisdiction in private international law and the state's human rights obligations in public international law. To the extent that international human rights treaties apply extraterritorially, states are duty-bound to ensure access to justice and effective civil remedies for third-country victims of corporate human rights abuses. To be able to enjoy the protection of their human rights in transnational tort litigations against MNCs, victims of corporate human rights abuses need to come within the human rights jurisdiction of the state concerned.

Jurisdiction in private international law determines the competence of state courts to hear private disputes involving a foreign element. In most general terms, the determining factor is whether there exists a sufficiently close nexus between the facts of the case and the forum state. In EU law, this nexus is established through the domicile of the defendant in an EU Member State. The allocation of jurisdiction in private international law serves a number of different purposes, such as protecting the legitimate interest of private parties in cross-border disputes, ensuring an economical judicial process, and avoiding conflicting judgments in different states. Yet it is also an expression of the delimitation of jurisdiction in public international law that protects the state's sovereign authority over its territory and people therein against undue external interference by other states. Jurisdiction in public international law regulates states' legal competence to assert authority in matters not exclusively of domestic concern, in accordance with a recognized legal basis and subject to a standard of reasonableness. It is commonly divided into prescriptive jurisdiction (the state's authority to prescribe legal rules), enforcement jurisdiction (the state's authority to enforce legal rules), and adjudicative jurisdiction (the authority of state courts to adjudicate disputes referred to them).[7] This entails, as Crawford notes, that 'the starting point in this part of the law is the presumption that jurisdiction (in all its forms) is territorial, and may not be exercised

6 *Ibid.*, paras 69, 95.

7 The latter category is sometimes subsumed under the state's prescriptive and enforcement jurisdiction, see V. Lowe, 'Jurisdiction' in M. Evans (ed.), *International Law* (2003) 329, 333.

extra-territorially without some specific basis in international law'.[8] Moreover, it suggests that the competence of state courts in private international law to hear disputes involving extraterritorial corporate human rights abuses is constrained by the state's jurisdiction under public international law.[9]

The way in which public international law constrains states' jurisdictional competences to assert legal authority outside their borders has also informed debates about the extraterritorial application of international human rights treaties. The text of Article 1 ECHR does not suggest that human rights jurisdiction should be delimited by state territory but simply provides that 'the High Contracting Parties shall secure to everyone within their jurisdiction the rights and freedoms defined in . . . this Convention'. Nevertheless, according to the ECtHR, 'jurisdiction is presumed to be exercised normally throughout the State's territory' and 'acts of the Contracting States performed, or producing effects, outside their territories can constitute an exercise of jurisdiction within the meaning of Article 1 only in exceptional circumstances'.[10] Whether acts performed, or producing effects, outside the state's territory bring an individual under that state's human rights jurisdiction for the purpose of triggering corresponding extraterritorial human rights obligations depends on the establishment of a qualified relationship of power and control between the state and the individual victim. Importantly, whether a state asserts power and control over an individual outside its borders is established independently of whether that state was legally competent in public international law to exercise jurisdiction on the territory of another state.[11] According to the ECtHR, the decisive factor for establishing a 'jurisdictional link' between the applicants and the respondent state is not the (il)legality of state action but the state's exercise of power and control, whether directly or indirectly, over foreign territory and people therein.[12] Similarly, the UN Human Rights Committee considers that 'a state party must respect and ensure the rights laid down in the [International Covenant on Civil

8 J. Crawford, *Brownlie's Principles of Public International Law* (2012, 8th ed.) 456.

9 Although it should be noted that the risk of civil courts unduly interfering with the sovereignty of other states by assuming jurisdiction over extraterritorial corporate human rights violations is mitigated in those cases that are decided according to the substantive law of the third state, see O. de Schutter, 'Extraterritorial Jurisdiction as a tool for improving the Human Rights Accountability of Transnational Corporations' (2006). Accessible at http://business-humanrights.org/en/pdf-extraterritorial-jurisdiction-as-a-tool-for-improving-the-human-rights-accountability-of-transnational-corporations.

10 ECtHR (Grand Chamber), *Al-Skeini and Others v United Kingdom* (Judgment of 7 July 2011) para. 131.

11 The implications of this difference between establishing jurisdiction in general public international law and international human rights law are further elaborated in D. Augenstein and D. Kinley, 'Beyond the 100 Acre Wood: in which international human rights law finds new ways to tame global corporate power', 19(6) *The International Journal of Human Rights* (2015) 828–848.

12 *Al Skeini and Others v United Kingdom* (Judgment of 7 July 2011) paras 136–138.

and Political Rights] to anyone within [its] power or effective control . . . even if not situated within the territory of the state party . . . and regardless of the circumstances in which such power or effective control was obtained'.[13] Accordingly, as per the Inter-American Commission of Human Rights, 'the inquiry turns not on the presumed victim's nationality or presence within a particular geographic area, but on whether, under the specific circumstances, the state observed the rights of a person subject to its authority and control'.[14]

Foreign victims of corporate human rights abuses also come under the 'authority and control' and therewith the human rights jurisdiction of an EU Member State by bringing legal proceedings in the domestic courts of that Member State. In *White v Sweden*, for example, the applicant living in Mozambique complained that two publications in Swedish newspapers associating him with various crimes (including the murder of Prime Minister Olof Palme) violated his right to private and family life as protected by Article 8 ECHR.[15] Before turning to the Strasbourg court, Mr White had brought a private prosecution for defamation against the newspapers in Sweden. The responsible editors were acquitted by a Swedish District Court, a judgment that was upheld on appeal. Without further ado, the ECtHR considered the applicant to be within Sweden's jurisdiction for the purpose of Article 1 ECHR and simply noted that 'this complaint is not manifestly ill-founded . . . [nor] inadmissible on any other grounds.[16]

The ECHR does not directly provide for a right of foreign victims to bring civil proceedings against MNCs in a European Member State. However, when victims of corporate human rights abuses attempt to bring such proceedings, EU Member State courts deciding on their jurisdiction under private international law must have due regard to their human rights obligations to ensure access to justice under Article 6 ECHR. This was confirmed by the ECtHR Grand Chamber judgment in *Markovic* – a case that concerned the attempt of applicants from Serbia and Montenegro to bring civil proceedings in Italy for human rights abuses committed during a NATO airstrike in Belgrade in 1999.[17] The Italian courts declined jurisdiction because the claimants were not entitled under Italian law to seek reparation from the Italian state for civil damages incurred as a result of a violation of public international law. The ECtHR, by contrast, unanimously held that the claimants came under the Italy's human

13 HRC *General Comment No. 31: The Nature of the General Legal Obligation Imposed on States Parties to the Covenant*, CCPR/C/21/Rev.1/Add.13, 26 May 2004, 10.
14 IACHR, *Coard et al v The United States* (Judgment of 29 September 1999) para. 37.
15 ECtHR, *White v Sweden* (Judgment of 19 December 2006).
16 *Ibid.*, para. 16.
17 ECtHR (Grand Chamber), *Markovic and Others v Italy* (Judgment of 14 December 2006). The case concerned the same facts as the ECtHR's previous admissibility decision in *Banković* (see ECtHR, *Banković & Others v Belgium & Others* (Admissibility Decision of 12 December 2001).

rights jurisdiction and could therefore benefit from the state's obligation to ensure access to justice (Article 6 ECHR):

> If the domestic law recognises a right to bring an action and if the right claimed is one which prima facie possesses the characteristics required by Article 6 of the Convention, the Court sees no reason why such domestic proceedings should not be subjected to the same level of scrutiny as any other proceedings brought at the national level. Even though the extraterritorial nature of the events alleged to have been at the origin of an action may have an effect on the applicability of Article 6 and the final outcome of the proceedings, it cannot under any circumstances affect the jurisdiction *ratione loci* and *ratione personae* of the State concerned. If civil proceedings are brought in the domestic courts, the State is required by Article 1 of the Convention to secure in those proceedings respect for the rights protected by Article 6. The Court considers that, once a person brings a civil action in the courts or tribunals of a State, there indisputably exists, without prejudice to the outcome of the proceedings, a 'jurisdictional link' for the purpose of Article 1.[18]

At the merits stage, the court gave some further indication as to what is required by the European Convention in such cases. On the one hand, Article 6 ECHR extends only to disputes over civil rights and obligations 'which can be said, at least on arguable grounds, to be recognised under domestic law; it does not itself guarantee any particular content for (civil) rights and obligations in the substantive law of the Contracting States'.[19] Yet on the other hand,

> [it] would not be consistent with the rule of law in a democratic society or with the basic principle underlying Article 6 § 1 – namely that civil claims must be capable of being submitted to a judge for adjudication – if, for example, a State could, without restraint or control by the Convention enforcement bodies, remove from the jurisdiction of the courts a whole range of civil claims or immunities or confer immunities from civil liability on large groups or categories of persons.[20]

Moreover, while Article 6 ECHR does not oblige EU Member States to create any particular remedy, 'it can be relied upon by anyone who considers that an interference with the exercise of one of his (civil) rights is unlawful and complains that he has not had the possibility of submitting that claim to a tribunal meeting the requirements of Article 6 § 1'.[21]

18 *Ibid.*, paras 53, 54.
19 *Ibid.*, para. 93.
20 *Ibid.*, para. 97.
21 *Ibid.*, para. 98.

Various comments and concluding observations of the UN Treaty Bodies also suggest that states have obligations under international human rights law to prevent and redress abuses committed by MNCs on the territory of another state.[22] In its well known General Comment No. 14 on the Right to Health, for instance, the Committee on Economic, Social and Cultural Rights (CESCR) called upon states 'to respect the enjoyment of the right to health in other countries, and to prevent third parties from violating the right in other countries, if they are able to influence these third parties by way of legal or political means, in accordance with the Charter of the United Nations and applicable international law'.[23] The Committee's General Comment on social security provides that 'state parties should extraterritorially protect the right to social security by preventing their own citizens and national entities from violating this right in other countries'.[24] In 2011, CESCR adopted a 'Statement of the obligations of states parties regarding the corporate sector and economic, social and cultural rights' in which it called upon states to 'take steps to prevent human rights contraventions abroad by companies which have their main seat under their jurisdiction, without infringing the sovereignty or diminishing the obligations of the host states under the Covenant'.[25] Similarly, the Committee on the Rights of the Child considers that home states 'have obligations . . . to respect, protect and fulfil children's rights in the context of businesses' extraterritorial activities and operations, provided that there is a reasonable link between the state and the conduct concerned'.[26]

Once again, these obligations encompass the prevention and redress of extraterritorial corporate human rights abuses. In its Concluding Observations on Germany, for example, the Human Rights Committee showed itself concerned that measures taken by the state to provide remedies against German companies violating human rights abroad 'may not be sufficient in all cases'. Accordingly, the Committee encouraged Germany 'to take appropriate measures to strengthen the remedies provided to protect people who have been victims of activities of such business enterprises operating abroad'.[27] Similarly, in its Concluding Observations on the UK, the Committee on the Elimination of Racial Discrimination

22 For an overview and discussion of the relevant case law and treaty body commentary, see the 'Maastricht Principles on Extraterritorial Obligations of States in the Area of Economic, Social and Cultural Rights' (2011), published with extensive annotations in 34 *Human Rights Quarterly* (2012) 1084–1169.

23 CESCR, *General Comment No. 14: The Right to the Highest Attainable Standard of Health*, E/C.12/2000/4 (11 August 2000) para. 39.

24 CESCR, *General Comment 19: The Right to Social Security*, E/C.12/GC/19 (4 February 2008) 54.

25 CESCR, *Statement on the obligations of States Parties regarding the corporate sector and economic, social and cultural rights*, E/C.12/2011/1 (12 July 2011) para. 5.

26 CRC, *General Comment 16 on State obligations regarding the impact of the business sector on children's rights*, CRC/C/CG/16 (17 April 2013) 43.

27 HRC, *Concluding observations on the sixth periodic report of Germany, adopted by the Committee at its 106th session*, 15 October to 2 November (2012) para. 16.

(CERD) recommended that 'the state party should ensure that no obstacles are introduced in the law that prevent the holding of transnational companies accountable in the state party's courts when such abuses are committed outside the state party'.[28] CERD has also called on the US and Canada to explore ways to hold business entities incorporated in their jurisdiction accountable for extra-territorial violations of the Covenant.[29]

To conclude, the ECHR imposes obligations on EU Member States to ensure access to justice and effective remedies in civil proceedings brought by victims of human rights abuses committed by MNCs within their human rights jurisdiction. Moreover, whenever third-country victims of corporate human rights abuses attempt to bring civil proceedings in an EU Member State court, they come within that Member State's human rights jurisdiction with the consequence that the court has to interpret private international law in the light of the state's human rights obligations under Article 6 ECHR.

1.3 Jurisdiction in private international law in Europe and the US

1.3.1 Introduction

This section outlines the EU regulation of jurisdiction in private international law and compares it with the approach of the US. In the EU, the allocation of civil jurisdiction to Member State courts has been harmonized by the Brussels I Regulation. This section outlines the general functioning of, and the rationale behind, the Brussels I Regulation. To get a better understanding of Member States' views of human rights issues involved and how they should be addressed, the policy debate leading up to the reform of Brussels I (recast) will be discussed, with particular reference to questions of jurisdiction in the business and human rights context.[30] This is followed by a comparative discussion of the US approach to jurisdiction in private international law, including the Alien Tort Claims Act. This brief discussion of the developments in the US is promoted by the fact that until recently most business and human rights litigation took place before US domestic courts.

28 CERD, *Concluding observations: United Kingdom of Great Britain and Northern Ireland*, CRD/C/GBR/CO/18–20 (14 September 2011) para. 29.

29 CERD, *Concluding Observations: United States*, CERD/C/USA/CO/6 (8 May 2008) para. 30; CERD, *Concluding Observations: Canada*, CERD/C/CAN/CO/18 (25 May 2007) para. 17.

30 The focus of analysis is on non-contractual (tort) disputes as the most pertinent type of cases in the business and human rights domain. Accordingly, specific rules pertaining to contractual disputes such as choice of court clauses and consumer protection shall not be discussed.

1.3.2 The European approach: the Brussels I Regulation

In the EU, rules on jurisdiction in civil cases are partially harmonized through Regulation (EU) No. 1215/2012 of the European Parliament and of the Council 12 December 2012 on jurisdiction and the recognition and enforcement of judgments in civil and commercial matters (recast), OJ 2012 L 351/1, also known as the Brussels-I or Brussels-I bis Regulation.[31] Together with the Lugano Convention on jurisdiction and the recognition and enforcement of judgments in civil and commercial matters of 30 October 2007,[32] this Regulation forms the so-called Brussels regime on jurisdiction, recognition and enforcements of judgments in the EU. This regime contains some of the most important rules for establishing jurisdiction in tort cases for corporate human rights abuses.

1.3.2.1 Scope of application

According to Article 1(1), the Regulation applies *ratione materiae* to all civil and commercial disputes regardless of the court or tribunal, bar matters of revenue, customs or administrative disputes, or acts of states in exercise of their authority. Article 1(2) further exempts several other procedures, including family law,[33] social security, and bankruptcy. According to Article 4(1), the Regulation applies *ratione personae* to all procedures against persons domiciled in one of the EU Member States; conversely, in procedures against persons not domiciled in an EU Member State, in principle, the national rules on jurisdiction of the state where the cases is brought apply.[34] Whether a defendant is domiciled in a Member State is determined by that member state's law on residence whereas, pursuant to Article 63, companies are considered to be domiciled in the place where they have their statutory seat, central administration, or principal place of business. This is particularly relevant for the business and human rights context, considering the Regulation only applies against those entities in the corporate network that are domiciled in the EU. For the rest, it will be up to the law of the Member State whose courts are seized for the claim.

31 This regulation displaced Regulation No. 44/2001 (Council Regulation (EC) No. 44/2001 of 22 December 2000 on jurisdiction and the recognition and enforcement of judgments in civil and commercial matters (Brussels I) OJ [2001] L 12/1 on 10 January 2015, which in turn superseded the Brussels Convention of 27 September 1968 on Jurisdiction and the Enforcement of Judgments in Civil and Commercial Matters.

32 Extending the rules of the Brussels I Regulation to Denmark, Iceland, Norway and Switzerland.

33 Covered by Council Regulation (EC) No. 2201/2003 concerning jurisdiction and the recognition and enforcement of judgments in matrimonial matters and the matters of parental responsibility (Brussels II Bis).

34 See further below, section four.

1.3.2.2 Rules on jurisdiction

The Regulation's main purposes are the promotion of free circulation of judgments within the Union,[35] and in pursuance of that goal, creating the highest possible degree of legal certainty.[36] The cornerstone of the Brussels I Regulation is Article 4(1) which determines both applicability of the Regulation and the main ground for jurisdiction, holding that persons domiciled in a Member State shall be sued in the courts of that Member State. For legal persons, domicile is determined by Article 63(1), where domicile is defined as the state where a company or other legal person has its statutory seat,[37] central administration or principal place of business. As the Brussels I Regulation is a closed system that harmonizes Member States' rules on jurisdiction within its scope of application, Member State courts are barred from considering grounds of jurisdiction other than those contained within Brussels I. Courts are equally prevented from dismissing cases on grounds other than those contained in the Regulation, as was clarified by the European Court of Justice (ECJ) with regard to the non-applicability of *forum non conveniens* in *Owusu v Jackson*.[38] Consequently, in cases against corporate entities, even when the acts occurred extraterritorially, the courts of a Member State will in principle have jurisdiction over the entity that is incorporated on that Member State's territory.

Brussels I contains some additions and exceptions to that basic rule, described in sections 2–7 of the Regulation. Most relevant for the business and human rights context is the additional ground under Article 7(2), giving concurrent jurisdiction in cases of tort, delict or quasi-delict to the courts of the Member State where the tort was committed, and the state where the harm occurred. Additionally, Article 7(3) grants concurrent jurisdiction to the courts of the Member State where the same act has already given rise to criminal proceedings. Other exceptions are less relevant to tort cases in the business and human rights area, such as jurisdiction of the courts of the place of performance of a contractual obligation, jurisdiction in disputes over immovable property, or specific rules in situations where parties have mutually agreed to a specific forum. Such agreements will, however, not occur, or only rarely, in cases related to business and human rights.

As the Regulation only applies to companies domiciled in the EU, it generally does not apply in tort cases against subsidiaries, save for two possibilities. First,

35 P. Jenard, Report on the Convention on jurisdiction and the enforcement of judgments in civil and commercial matters signed at Brussels, 27 September 1968. *Official Journal* C 59, 5 March 1979.

36 ECJ 17 June 1992 – C-26/91, *Handte v TMCS* [1992] ECR I 3967.

37 As indicated by Art. 63(2), not all EU Member States have a concept of statutory seat, in which case the registered office, place, or law of incorporation of the company works.

38 ECJ 1 March 2005 – C-281/02 *Owusu v Jackson* [2005] ECR I-01383, holding that a court cannot decline jurisdiction on the basis of *forum non conveniens* in cases that fall within the ambit of Brussels I.

some states apply the same tests when determining residual jurisdiction in their domestic law as the ECJ applies with comparable provisions of the Regulation, of their own volition. Such was the case in the Dutch *Akpan v Shell* case,[39] where foreseeability of the joining of claims against the parent and subsidiary was assessed according to the ECJ's criteria in *Painer*.[40] Regulation standards may thus be relevant beyond its formal scope of application. In this case, the ECJ ruled that joining defendants when there are different legal bases for the claims against them is possible under Art. 6(1) (old) of the Regulation, provided it was foreseeable by the defendants that they might be sued in a Member State where at least one of them is domiciled.[41] This test only applies when a case falls within the scope of the Regulation, but as in *Akpan*, Member State courts have applied similar tests to cases not decided under the Regulation, to avoid creating a gap between Regulation and non-Regulation standards.

Second, the Regulation may apply directly to a third state-incorporated subsidiary when a plaintiff can prove that a subsidiary's central administration lies with its parent company, rather than in its state of incorporation. Such was argued in *Vava and others v AASA*,[42] in the absence of ECJ decisions on the subject. The argument was rejected in that specific case, but could hypothetically be raised in a subsequent case. If accepted, the Regulation would apply and the court of the state of incorporation of the parent may have jurisdiction. This is, however, hard to argue as it requires extensive knowledge of the corporate group's decision-making process and internal organization, and the concept of central administration has thus far been scarcely defined absent an ECJ ruling on the matter. This problem is tackled in recommendation no. 5.

1.3.2.3 Policy debate regarding the reform of the Brussels I Regulation

As mentioned, the current Regulation is a recast version of the previous Regulation 44/2001. While the core principles have not changed significantly, the Commission's initial proposal for a new Regulation was much more ambitious.[43] While the most far-reaching proposals were dropped following negotiations with the Member States and Parliament amendments, that rejection is informative in other aspects for the business and human rights debate. It is worth noting that the recasting process was, amongst other concerns, also prompted by a

39 *Akpan v Shell*, ECLI:NL:RBSGR:2013:BY9854 (30 January 2013).

40 ECJ 1 December 2011 – C-145/10, *Eva-Maria Painer v Standard VerlagsGmbH and Others* [2011] ECLI:EU:C:2011:798.

41 *Ibid.*, para. 81.

42 *Vava v Anglo American South Africa Ltd (No 2)* [2013] EWHC 2131 (QB).

43 Green Paper on the Review of Council Regulation (EC) No. 44/2001 on Jurisdiction and the Recognition and Enforcement of Judgments in Civil and Commercial Matters, Brussels, 21.4.2009, COM(2009) 174 final. Accessible at http://eur-lex.europa.eu/LexUriServ/LexUriServ.do?uri=COM:2009:0175:FIN:EN:PDF.

discussion of how the Brussels I regime functions in the international legal order and relates to third states.[44]

Because the regime only extends to defendants domiciled in an EU Member State, EU citizens can experience unequal access to justice depending on whether their claim is against an EU-based defendant or a defendant domiciled in a third state, over which the forum state courts may or may not have jurisdiction under national law. Such a situation could also occur in business and human rights cases, where a national court may have jurisdiction over a parent company incorporated on its territory, but not over a subsidiary incorporated in a third state where the harm also occurred. As a possible remedy for this inequality, the Commission initially suggested extending its rules to non-EU defendants, fully harmonizing the Member States' rules on jurisdiction in civil and commercial disputes. This would have brought Brussels I in line with the Rome I and II Regulations on applicable law that claim universal application in their respective areas.[45] It would have also barred the application of national rules on residual jurisdiction currently in force in the Member States. To compensate, the Regulation would have included two additional grounds of jurisdiction, *forum necessitatis*/forum of necessity (Article 26) and asset-based jurisdiction (Article 25). The former would have provided for jurisdiction where it is impossible or unreasonable for the claimant to bring a case in another state.[46] The latter concerns jurisdiction in cases where the defendant owns property in the forum state, provided the value of that property is not disproportionate to the claim – as currently present in German and Austrian civil law.[47]

Both grounds for jurisdiction would have facilitated tort litigations for extraterritorial corporate human rights abuses in EU Member State courts: *forum necessitatis* jurisdiction because it aims at preventing a denial of justice, asset-based jurisdiction because it facilitates litigation in states where a company does significant business without having its statutory seat or head office there. These proposals were not, however, included in the final proposal to the European Parliament; in fact, universal application was dropped entirely. The European

44 See Green Paper on the Review of Council Regulation (EC) No. 44/2001 on Jurisdiction and the Recognition and Enforcement of Judgments in Civil and Commercial Matters, Brussels, 21.4.2009, COM(2009) 174 final. Accessible at http://eur-lex.europa.eu/LexUriServ/LexUriServ.do?uri=COM:2009:0175:FIN:EN:PDF; Green Paper on the Brussels I Regulation, House of Lords European Union Committee, 21st Report, Session 2008–2009. Accessible at http://ec.europa.eu/justice/newsroom/civil/opinion/files/090630/ms_parliaments/united_kingdom_house_of_lords_en.pdf.

45 See Rome I, Art. 2; Rome II, Art. 3.

46 See further below, section four.

47 See Code of Civil Procedure as promulgated on 5 December 2005 (Bundesgesetzblatt (BGBl., Federal Law Gazette) I page 3202; 2006 I page 431; 2007 I page 1781), last amended by Article 1 of the Act dated 10 October 2013 (Federal Law Gazette I page 3786), s. 23; Julian Feichtinger and Karin Lehner, *Comparative Study of Residual Jurisdiction in Civil and Commercial Disputes in the EU, National Report for Austria*. Accessible at http://ec.europa.eu/civiljustice/news/docs/study_resid_jurisd_austria_en.pdf.

Parliament expressed concern that the Commission had overstepped its mandate by proposing to extend the scope of the Regulation and thereby significantly changing its meaning and effect. The Parliament felt that a much wider range of consultations and debate should have taken place before taking that step. Moreover, it considered that a unilateral move on the part of the EU would 'not necessarily improve' the EU's positions in future negotiations regarding a worldwide jurisdiction and judgments convention.[48]

While few states publicly expressed their opinion on the Commission's proposal, one can find some explanation for the rejection of the proposal in the Dutch response, which was quite comprehensive. The arguments underlying this response can be found in an advisory opinion from the joint Dutch advisory committees on Private International Law and Civil Law, which was followed by the Minister of Justice and both parliamentary chambers.[49] These committees advised that full harmonization of jurisdiction rules with respect to defendants from third states was not desirable, for two reasons. First, as the issue would also affect non-EU legal orders, the committees felt that the EU should leave it to the Hague Conference for Private International Law rather than unilaterally extend its jurisdiction rules to affect cases from third states.

Second, in the Commissions' view, the Brussels I regime is distributive rather than attributive in nature. In other words, Brussels I was not meant to create new grounds for jurisdiction, but 'merely' to create a practical division of jurisdictional powers between the Member States – a road map for civil litigants. The rationale behind this regime is the EU principle of mutual trust in other Member States' legal systems, a principle that does not apply to third states. Consequently, there would be no guarantee that third state courts will assume jurisdiction where an EU State cannot; nor would an EU Member States' assumption of jurisdiction on the basis of the revised Brussels I regime under draft Articles 25 and 26 guarantee recognition and enforcement by the courts in the third states concerned. Thus, the committees concluded, the closed nature of the Brussels I regime does not lend itself to extension to disputes involving third state defendants.[50] While no other reasoned rebuttals were publicly submitted to the Commission's proposal, the fact that Articles 25 and 26 were omitted (and only specific protection for consumers and employees of third state defendants remained in the recast Regulation) suggests that the above arguments also resonated with other Member States in the closed negotiations. The UK Green Paper cited above suggested some changes to the original Regulation to accommodate differences in legal protection, yet most

48 Draft report on the proposal for a regulation of the European Parliament and of the Council on jurisdiction and the recognition and enforcement of judgments in civil and commercial matters (recast), PE467.046v01–00 [28 June 2011] (EP Draft Report).

49 Advies ontwerp-Verordening Brussel I (document COM (2010) 748 d.d. 14 december 2010), No. 5689654/11/6. Accessible at https://www.eerstekamer.nl/eu/publicatie/20110909/advies_ontwerp_verordening_brussel/document.

50 *Ibid.*

Member States resisted transferring more national competences on jurisdiction to the EU.

Two conclusions can be drawn from the recent recasting process of the Brussels I Regulation that bear relevance for the question of whether, in the view of the EU Member States, further modifications to the regime are needed to accommodate business and human rights concerns. First, the long and tedious process itself makes it highly unlikely that substantial modifications will be added in the near future. Moreover, the driving concern behind reviewing Brussels I was the removal of unequal legal protection of Community residents, rather than that of third-country nationals. Second, adding specific grounds for jurisdiction to facilitate transnational tort litigation for extraterritorial corporate human rights abuses would entail extending the scope of Brussels I scope to all civil cases, not just those involving EU-domiciled defendants – a proposal that has been categorically rejected by the Member States in the recasting process. Accordingly, and for the foreseeable future, the rules of jurisdiction governing third state defendants in cases for corporate human rights abuses will be those of the EU Member States. This may not be a bad thing. While the proposed Articles 25 and 26 in Brussels I Recast would have offered some possibility for recourse, they would also displace national rules of residual jurisdiction that may provide better opportunities in business and human rights cases.

1.3.3 The US approach to jurisdiction

Over the last two decades many victims of alleged corporate human rights abuses around the world have brought their cases before US domestic courts. As will be discussed, recent developments in the US have brought the US approach to jurisdiction more in line with the approach under the Brussels I regime. Most of the plaintiffs bringing their cases before US domestic courts have relied on the Alien Tort Statute (ATS).[51] In 2013, the US Supreme Court in *Kiobel v Royal Dutch Petroleum Co.*[52] restricted but did not eliminate federal jurisdiction over abuses of certain well-established rules of international law. A likely consequence is that litigants will increasingly rely on US general private international law and litigate their cases in US state courts under domestic tort law. The cause of action under the ATS (violations of the law of nations) will in many cases also constitute a violation of the law of the US forum.

The following sections will discuss several doctrines that have been developed in US case law, which courts consider in order to determine their competence. In practice, consideration of these doctrines has limited the access to US courts for plaintiffs in transnational cases. In the final section, the EU and US approach to jurisdiction is compared.

51 Alien Tort Statute (28 U.S.C. § 1350).
52 *Kiobel v Royal Dutch Petroleum Co.*, 133 SCt 1659 (2013).

1.3.3.1 Doctrines that may limit access to US courts in transnational cases

In this section the following doctrines, which are relevant for the issue of jurisdiction, are addressed: the requirements of personal jurisdiction, the presumption against extraterritoriality, *forum non conveniens*, and comity. The doctrines address different aspects of a court's power to hear a case: *forum non conveniens* and comity provide courts with a discretionary basis for declining to exercise jurisdiction; personal jurisdiction considers a court's adjudicative power over the defendant; and the presumption of extraterritoriality goes to the scope of a statutory cause of action (prescriptive jurisdiction). A case may be dismissed on other grounds, such aspolitical question and immunity, inter alia, but these will not be considered here.

Unlike the statutory approach in the EU, the US approach to jurisdiction has evolved through interpretation of statutes and the US Constitution (especially the Due Process Clause of the Fourteenth Amendment) by the US Supreme Court. Courts are required to make a factual determination each time in determining whether jurisdiction is in accordance with the requirements of due process. In US case law several doctrines have been developed that US courts will apply to determine their competence and may constitute a barrier for plaintiffs bringing a transnational human rights case. These doctrines address both questions of prescriptive and adjudicative jurisdiction. Over the last two decades, the US courts have become increasingly responsive to these doctrines, which all speak to the nexus between the US, the parties, and a given suit. The underlying rationale of these doctrines is the balancing of interests pro-defendant, international comity, and considerations of judicial efficiency and fairness.

1.3.3.2 The Alien Tort Statute: presumption against extraterritoriality and personal jurisdiction

The possibility of using the ATS in tort litigations for extraterritorial corporate human rights abuses has been limited by the recent US Supreme Court decisions in *Kiobel* and *Daimler AG v Baumann*[53] based on the doctrine presumption against extraterritoriality and the limitation of personal jurisdiction respectively and will thus be discussed in that context. The unique character of the ATS must be pointed out; no other state has any statute that is comparable in its scope and effects.

As stated above, most transnational human rights litigation has been brought before the US domestic courts under the ATS, the provision in the 1789 Judiciary Act that provides federal courts with jurisdiction over civil actions for 'a tort only, committed in violation of the law of nations or a treaty of the United States'. Until recently, US courts have accepted that a minimal connection to

53 *Daimler AG v Bauman* No. 11–965, 571 US (2014).

the US forum was sufficient to establish jurisdiction under the ATS. The result was hundreds of transnational human rights civil suits being brought before the US courts seeking monetary compensation for a broad range of human rights violations.

The question decided by the US Supreme Court in *Kiobel* was whether a claim brought under the ATS 'may reach conduct occurring in the territory of a foreign sovereign', even assuming that the conduct was performed by an individual or entity that subsequently came within the personal jurisdiction of a US court.[54] The *Kiobel* majority, by applying the presumption against extraterritoriality to the judicial creation of a cause of action under the ATS, curbed the remedial reach of this jurisdictional statute. According to the US Supreme Court, the presumption can only be overcome if the claim 'touches and concerns' the Unites States 'with sufficient force'.[55] Whether this allows judges to create causes of action for conduct occurring exclusively in the territory of a foreign sovereign remains contested.[56] In his concurrence, Justice Breyer recognized three scenarios in which the exercise of US jurisdiction would be appropriate under the ATS, the first based on the principle of territoriality (if the tort occurred on American soil); the second based on the principle of nationality (if the defendant is an American national); and the third based on US national interest, including 'a distinct interest in preventing the United States from becoming a safe harbour (free of civil as well as criminal liability) for a torturer or other common enemy of mankind.'[57] However, this concurrence only has limited persuasive power.

Whether a case touches and concerns the US with sufficient force is for the lower courts to decide. In decisions post-*Kiobel*, lower courts have mainly followed the idea that cases against foreign companies for conduct abroad should be dismissed.[58] In July 2015, the District Court for the District of Colombia in the case *Doe I v Exxon Mobile* decided that the plaintiffs succeeded in showing that the case sufficiently 'touched and concerned' the US.[59] In this case the plaintiffs alleged that Exxon Mobile should be held liable for aiding and abetting human rights abuses committed by members of the Indonesian military. The military was providing security for the company in Indonesia in 2000 and 2001. The jurisdictional hook was found in US-based decision-making by executives of the company.

54 *Kiobel v Royal Dutch Petroleum Co.*, 133 SCt 1659 (2013) 1664.

55 *Ibid.*, 1669.

56 Maria Chiara Marullo and Francisco Javier Zamora Cabot, *Transnational Human Rights Litigations. Kiobel's* Touch and Concern*: A Test Under Construction*, April 2016. Accessible at http://papers.ssrn.com/sol3/Papers.cfm?abstract_id=2765068.

57 *Ibid.*, 1671.

58 Maria Chiara Marullo and Francisco Javier Zamora Cabot, *Transnational Human Rights Litigations. Kiobel's* Touch and Concern: *A Test Under Construction*, April 2016. Accessible at http://papers.ssrn.com/sol3/Papers.cfm?abstract_id=2765068.

59 *Doe v ExxonMobil Corp.* (DDC July 6, 2015).

To ascertain personal jurisdiction, US courts will consider whether defendants' contacts with the forum are sufficiently 'continuous and systematic' to render it subject to the forum jurisdiction. The courts will address the question whether jurisdiction is 'reasonable'.[60] This contacts-based analysis of jurisdiction resulted in a broad approach where multinational companies with offices in many countries could be sued in the US for conduct anywhere in the world. In January 2014, in *Daimler AG v Bauman* the US Supreme Court asserted that ATS litigation should satisfy a stricter general jurisdiction requirement.[61] In this case, the plaintiffs, twenty-three Argentine citizens, sought to establish personal jurisdiction in a Californian federal court against the German parent company Daimler AG based upon the presence in California of two Mercedes Benz marketing offices. They alleged that the Argentine military, which had ruled the country from 1976 to 1983, brutalized, tortured, or murdered them or their close relatives. They further alleged that Mercedes Benz Argentina had aided and abetted the military in these human rights violations. The Supreme Court in *Daimler* said that a defendant is subject to 'general jurisdiction' only if its extensive contacts with the forum render it 'at home' there.[62] To satisfy this requirement, the courts will consider the places where a company is incorporated and where it maintains its principal place of business. It did not 'foreclose the possibility' that there might exist an 'exceptional case' in which a company's contacts with a third state were 'so substantial and of such a nature as to render the company at home in the State'.[63] The 'at home' standard will probably exclude from US courts most cases concerning conduct abroad by foreign defendants that are not incorporated in the US (foreign cubed cases). Specific jurisdiction, i.e. where a forum is alleged to have jurisdiction over a defendant because the defendant's activities in that forum gave rise to the claim itself, is still available against foreign defendants.

1.3.3.3 Further doctrines that may limit access to US courts in transnational cases

In addition to the previously discussed presumption against extraterritorial application and the requirements of personal jurisdiction, the doctrines of *forum non conveniens* and comity are of particular relevance. Both *forum non conveniens* and comity provide courts with a discretionary basis for declining to exercise jurisdiction. A case may also be dismissed on other grounds such as political question and immunity but these will not be considered here. The *forum non*

60 For a discussion of the requirement of reasonablesness see Kate Bonacorssi, 'Not at home with "at home" jurisdiction', 37(6) *Fordham International Law Journal*, (2014) 1828–1830.

61 For an analysis of this case see F.J. Zamora Cabot, *Decision of the Supreme Court of the United States in the* Daimler AG v Bauman et al *case: closing the golden door*, April 2014. Accessible at: http://www.tiempodelosderechos.es/docs/wp-2–2014-englishversion.pdf.

62 *Daimler AG v Bauman* 134 SCt 751.

63 *Ibid.*, 761.

conveniens doctrine may preclude a case from coming to federal court when there is an alternative forum that is more appropriate as it is more closely linked with the case due to the location of parties, witnesses, evidence, and so on. *Forum non convenience* (like comity) is a discretionary, non-statutory doctrine developed mostly by trial courts. Courts in their *forum non conveniens* analysis are guided by private interests (focus on burden for defendant) and by public interests (especially judicial resources). It has been noted that courts have increasingly been granting *forum non conveniens* motions in cases involving foreign plaintiffs.[64] Comity plays an important role in transnational cases before US courts. According to the US Supreme Court comity concerns 'the recognition which one nation allows within its territory to the legislative, executive or judicial acts of another nation, having due regard both to international duty and convenience, and to the rights of its own citizens or of other persons who are under the protection of its laws.'[65] Comity considerations may prompt a court not to adjudicate a case that has, is or will be heard in a foreign court out of deference to the sovereignty of the other state.[66]

1.3.3.4 Litigating torts in state courts and/or under state law

In light of the procedural and substantive hurdles plaintiffs face since the *Kiobel* and *Daimler* decisions, an alternative for victims of corporate related human rights abuse may be to litigate in state courts and/or to apply state tort law. The cause of action under the ATS, violations of the law of nations will mostly also constitute a violation of the law of the forum state (wrongful death, assault, battery etc.). Alternatively, such claims may be for transitory torts applying the law of the host state depending on the choice of law analysis applied by the state court. A benefit of bringing a case before state courts is that some of the procedural doctrines discussed above are only applicable in federal courts. State courts do not have to recognize these doctrines. For example, many state courts do not recognize in the same manner the doctrine of *forum non conveniens.*[67] However, some of the federal procedural doctrines discussed above do not only apply in federal courts but also in state courts, or equivalent limiting doctrines are applied. As the personal jurisdiction requirements emanate from a constitutional rule derived from the Due Process Clause, these requirements govern all US courts. Moreover, the limits on the extraterritorial application of state statutes

64 See for example, Donald Earl Childress III, '*Forum Non Conveniens*: the search for a convenient forum in transnational cases' 32(1) *Virginia Journal of International Law* (2012) 157.

65 *Hilton v Guyot*, 159 US 113, 143 (1895).

66 For more on the doctrine of comity see Beth Stephens *et al.* (eds.) *International Human Rights Litigation in US Courts* (2008, 2nd revised edn.) 354 ff.

67 Donald Earl Childress III, 'The Alien Tort Statute, Federalism and the next wave of transnational litigation', 100 *Georgetown Law Journal* (2012)709; see pp. 741–751 for an analysis of potential obstacles for plaintiffs to overcome at the state level.

and state common law are unsettled.[68] Thus, also at the state level, plaintiffs face significant procedural hurdles when bringing transnational cases.

1.3.4 Comparing the EU and US approach to jurisdiction in private international law

When comparing the US and the EU approach to jurisdiction in civil litigation there are marked differences in the sources of the rules and the rationale underlying their creation. It has been argued that the US approach to jurisdiction is more pro-defendant and thus more restrictive for plaintiffs than the European jurisdiction.[69] However, it should be noted that the Brussels I regime is expressly designed with a presumption against plaintiffs, and centralizes the defendant's domicile as its main ground for jurisdiction. An important difference lies in the more flexible approach under the Due Process Clause by US courts, whereas the EU favours a 'one-size-fits-all' approach dictated by legal certainty pursuant to the Brussels I Regulation. The US courts have been a magnet for transnational human rights litigation due to the flexible approach that the courts have taken to the issue of jurisdiction. However, a relatively recent development can be witnessed whereby the US approach to jurisdiction in transnational cases shows a resurgence of territorially-based reasoning, increasingly pushing out transnational cases as evidenced in the two decisions discussed above: *Kiobel* and *Daimler*. The *Kiobel* decision limited subject matter jurisdiction in transnational human rights cases under the ATS. Since the *Daimler* decision the ability of courts to assert personal general jurisdiction over foreign companies in transnational cases has been restricted, bringing these more in line with internationally accepted standards of domicile. The retreat to reasoning based on territoriality to an extent brings the US approach closer to the criteria applied in the EU context to determine whether jurisdiction may be ascertained.

1.4 Residual jurisdiction in Europe

1.4.1 Introduction

The Brussels I Regulation (recast) only applies if the defendant is domiciled in a Member State (Article 4). A company is considered to be domiciled in a Member State if it has its statutory seat, its central administration, or its principal place of business there (Article 63). If none of these conditions is fulfilled (as will often be the case with subsidiaries and contractors of EU-based MNCs), the private international law of the Member States determines the jurisdiction of national courts (so-called residual jurisdiction). In this vein, Article 6 of the

68 *Ibid.*
69 See, for example, Kate Bonacorssi, 'Not at home with "at home jurisdiction"' 37(6) *Fordham International Law Journal* (2014) 1844.

Brussels I Regulation provides that 'if the defendant is not domiciled in a Member State, the jurisdiction of the courts of each Member State shall . . . be determined by the law of that Member State'. The following considerations discuss and illustrate three jurisdictional instruments in Member States' private international law that can facilitate tort litigations for human rights abuses committed by Europe-based MNCs: *forum necessitatis*, the joining of defendants, and the pursuit of civil remedies through criminal jurisdiction.

1.4.2 Forum necessitatis

The doctrine of *forum necessitatis* allows a court to accept jurisdiction in cases where there is no other forum available in which the plaintiff could pursue his/her claims. In the course of the 2009 review of the Brussels I Regulation, the European Commission proposed the inclusion of a *forum necessitatis* rule.[70] New Article 26 of the recast Brussels I Regulation would have provided that

> [w]here no court of a Member State has jurisdiction under the Regulation, the courts of a Member State may, on an exceptional basis, hear the case if the right to a fair trial or the right to access to justice so requires, in particular: (a) if proceedings cannot reasonably be brought or conducted or would be impossible in a third State with which the dispute is closely connected; or (b) if a judgment given on the claim in a third State would not be entitled to recognition and enforcement in the Member State of the court seized under the law of that State and such recognition and enforcement is necessary to ensure that the rights of the claimant are satisfied; and the dispute has a sufficient connection with the Member State of the Court seized.

The proposal was rendered obsolete because the proposed universal scope of the Regulation, for which this article functioned as a counterbalance, was rejected as described in paragraph 1.3.2.3. Nevertheless, *forum necessitatis* is still a recognized ground of jurisdiction in many EU Member States, either based in statute or developed through case law.[71] The conditions for *forum necessitatis* vary from Member State to Member State, yet it always constitutes an exceptional ground of jurisdiction. Claimants have to demonstrate that it is 'unreasonable' or 'unacceptable' to bring proceedings abroad. This may be due to legal obstacles (e.g. no guarantee of a fair trial in the third country) or practical obstacles, such as

70 *Commission Green Paper on the Review of Council Regulation (EC) No. 44/2001 on Jurisdiction and the Recognition and Enforcement of Judgments in Civil and Commercial Matters*, COM (2009) 175 final (21 April 2009); *Proposal for a Regulation of the European Parliament and of the Council on Jurisdiction and the Regulation and Enforcement of Judgments in Civil and Commercial Matters*, COM (2010) 748 final (14 December 2010).

71 For an overview see A. Nuyts, *Study on Residual Jurisdiction – General Report* (Brussels: 2007) 66.

that the claimant would in fact be deprived of an effective remedy. A further condition is usually that the claim has a sufficient connection with the Member State concerned.

Forum necessitatis jurisdiction is often considered to flow from, or even to be mandated by, Member States' human rights obligations under Article 6 ECHR. The 2009 Commission proposal to include *forum necessitatis* in the Brussels I Regulation made explicit reference to the 'right to a fair trial or the right to access to justice'. That jurisdiction 'of necessity' is based on or required by Article 6 ECHR was also considered in the course of parliamentary debates in a number of Member States, including Belgium and the Netherlands.[72] In other Member States, *forum necessitatis* is (in addition) linked to the prohibition of a denial of justice as a requirement of national constitutional law and a principle of public international law. Even in Member State jurisdictions such as England that do not explicitly recognize a forum of necessity, courts have considered that under exceptional circumstances a denial of the right to sue to foreign claimants could amount to a violation of Article 6 ECHR.[73] The following examples illustrate the importance of *forum necessitatis* jurisdiction in providing access to justice for victims of corporate-related human rights abuses committed outside the European Union.

Forum necessitatis jurisdiction has a statutory basis in Article 9 of the Dutch Code of Civil Procedure. Article 9 contains two different versions of the *forum necessitatis* rule, only one of which requires a connection to the Dutch forum. Dutch civil courts have accepted *forum necessitatis* jurisdiction in a case brought by Iraqi pilots residing in the Netherlands that concerned a labour dispute with the Kuwait Airlines Corporation.[74] Even though the labour contract established the competence of the Kuwaiti courts, the Dutch court accepted jurisdiction because the pilots, as former Iraqi nationals, could not expect a fair trial in Kuwait.[75] In the Palestinian Doctor case, the District Court of The Hague heard the claim of a Palestinian doctor for damages suffered from being unlawfully imprisoned in Libya because he had allegedly infected children with HIV/AIDS.[76] *Forum necessitatis* jurisdiction was justified having regard to the general political situation in Libya during that time, and irrespective of the fact that the claimant did not reside in the Netherlands.

72 *Ibid.*, 64.

73 *Mark v Mark* [2004] EWCA Civ 168, [2005] Fam 267.

74 *Abood/Kuwait Airways Corp.*, Amsterdam Sub-District Court (5 January 1996), 1996 Nederlands Internationaal Privaatrecht 145, 222 (Kuwait Airways case I).

75 In a similar case brought a few years later, the Dutch courts declined *forum necessitatis* jurisdiction due to an insufficient connection to the Dutch forum because the claimants did not reside in the Netherlands; see *Saloum/Kuwait Airways Corp.*, Amsterdam Sub-District Court (27 April 2000), 2000 Nederlands Internationaal Privaatrecht 315, 472 (Kuwait Airways case II).

76 *El-Hojouj/Unnamed Libyan Officials*, The Hague District Court (21 March 2012) LJN: BV9748.

There are cases in which French and Spanish courts have recognised *forum necessitatis* jurisdiction in the light of Article 6 ECHR and the prohibition of a denial of justice.[77] Spain has recently amended its private international law to include a statutory basis for *forum necessitatis*, which requires that the case has a sufficient link to the Spanish forum and that other courts connected with the dispute have declined jurisdiction.[78] In the COMILOG case, denial of justice was used to gain access to French courts.[79] In 1991, the Gabonese mining company COMILOG, operating on the territory of the Democratic Republic of Congo, laid off 955 workers without due notice or compensation. In 1992, the workers attempted to challenge their dismissal before a Congolese court that, however, failed to deliver a judgment. In 2003, COMILOG reached an agreement with the governments of Congo and Gabon according to which the company would compensate the workers who, in turn, were to renounce their right to a judicial remedy in relation to their unfair dismissal.[80] The workers claimed that they were not consulted about this agreement and did not receive the promised compensation. Meanwhile, the French company ERAMET had become the majority owner of COMILOG. In 2007, former COMILOG workers brought a complaint before a French employment tribunal, alleging unfair dismissal and requesting 65 million euros in compensation. While the employment tribunal dismissed the action for lack of jurisdiction, the Paris Court of Appeal held that French courts were competent to hear the case against COMILOG France and COMILOG International.[81] French jurisdiction was justified having regard to the necessity of avoiding a denial of justice to the Congolese workers. Moreover, that ERAMET was a French company was considered to establish a sufficiently close link to the French forum. In January 2015, the *Cour de Cassation* confirmed the jurisdiction of the French courts.[82] In September 2015,

77 See, respectively, *Vid.* Aix-en-Provence Court of Appeal (31 May 1923), JDI 1924, 204; *Vid.* Paris Court of Appeal (10 November 1960), JDI 1961, 426; and *Murcia Court of Appeals* (decision of 12 May 2003); *Madrid Commercial Court N. 1* (order of 5 July 2013).

78 Art. 22 octies 3. Art. 22.3 Organic Law 7/2015, of 21 July, whereby the Organic Law 6/1985, on the Judiciary Power (LOPJ) is modified.

79 On the background of the case see Sherpa, 'Affaire COMILOG: Victoire pour les 857 travailleurs victims d'un déni de justice', September 2015. Accessible at http://www.asso-sherpa.org/affaire-comilog-victoire-pour-les-857-travailleurs-victimes-dun-deni-de-justice#.Vjtg227zkhw.

80 See further ILO, *Report of the Committee set up to examine the representation made by the International Organization of Energy and Mines (OIEM) under article 24 of the ILO Constitution alleging non-observance by Congo of the Protection of Wages Convention, 1949 (No. 95)*. Accessible at http://www.ilo.org/dyn/normlex/en/f?p=1000:50012:0::NO::P50012_LANG_CODE:en:NO.

81 Cour d'appel de Paris (Pôle 6 – Chambre 2), du 20 juin 2013.

82 Cour de Cassation, civile, Chambre Sociale, 28 janvier 2015, 13–22.994 13–22.995 13–23.003 13–23.004 13–23.005 13–23.006.

the Paris Court of Appeal ordered COMILOG to compensate the workers for their unfair dismissal in Congo in 1992.[83]

1.4.3 Joining of defendants

One of the problems faced by litigants in tort litigations for corporate human rights abuses committed outside the European Union is that, while the parent company will often be domiciled in an EU Member State and thus fall under the Brussels I Regulation, the same is not true of the subsidiary or contractor that has committed the tortuous act. One way to overcome jurisdictional hurdles in relation to the subsidiary/contractor domiciled outside the EU is to join the proceedings against the parent and the subsidiary/contractor in a Member State court. Article 8(1) Brussels I Regulation permits the joining of defendants under the condition that 'the claims are so closely connected that it is expedient to hear and determine them together to avoid the risk of irreconcilable judgments resulting from separate proceedings'. The ECJ has made the joining of defendants under Article 8 subject to two conditions: the parent company cannot be sued with the exclusive aim of bringing the foreign subsidiary/contractor within the European jurisdiction; and a prior relation must exist between the defendants to be joined – a condition that will always be fulfilled when suing a corporate group.[84] Article 8 Brussels I Regulation only applies to defendants domiciled in an EU Member State, which relegates the question of whether proceedings against non-EU defendants can be joined to the residual jurisdiction of the Member States. In a number of Member States it is possible to join proceedings against EU and non-EU domiciled defendants, which facilitates tort litigation in the EU for human rights abuses committed by foreign subsidiaries or contractors of Europe-based MNCs.

A recent amendment of the Spanish private international law permits Spanish courts to join proceedings against foreign defendants provided at least one of the defendants is domiciled in Spain and the claims against the different defendants are sufficiently connected.[85] The following case, which is hypothetical though inspired by real events,[86] illustrates some of the reasons that may compel a Spanish court to join defendants in litigation for human rights abuses

83 Cour d'Appel de Paris, Arrêt du 10 Septembre 2015, S11/05955 S11/05956 S/1105957 S11/05958 S11/05959 S11/05960.

84 STJUE C-145/10 and C-616/10. See Virgós Soriano / Garcimartín Alférez, Derecho Procesal Civil Internacional. Litigación Internacional, Civitas, Madrid, 2007, pp. 214–215.

85 The amendment of the LOPJ provides that '*En caso de pluralidad de demandados, serán competentes los Tribunales españoles cuando al menos uno de ellos tenga su domicilio en España, siempre que se ejercite una sola acción o varias entre las que exista un nexo por razón del título o causa de pedir que aconsejen su acumulación*'. See Art. 22 ter 3. of the Organic Law 7/2015, of 21 july, whereby the Organic Law 6/1985, on the Judiciary Power (LOPJ) is modified.

86 See further ECCHR, *Holding Companies Accountable: Lessons from Transnational Human Rights Litigation* (2014).

committed by foreign subsidiaries of parent companies domiciled in Spain. GES.CO is the Colombian subsidiary of GEC, a Spanish energy company that produces electricity and distributes it to end consumers. In summer 2012, a short circuit in an electricity grid in a poor neighbourhood of Bogota maintained by GES.CO caused a fire that killed a number of inhabitants and destroyed their properties. The short circuit was allegedly the result of poor maintenance work by GES.CO. The Spanish parent company was implicated in the ensuing human rights abuses because it was under a legal obligation in Spanish law to ensure minimum quality standards in the provision of maintenance services by its subsidiary. Moreover, when incorporating in Colombia, GES.CO had made a commitment to meet the safety standards set by Colombian domestic law. Finally, not only did part of the capital of the subsidiary come from Spain but also its directors and members of the technical staff were delegated from the Spanish parent company. These various linkages between the companies, their alleged joined legal liability for the human rights abuses committed in Colombia, as well as the legitimate interest of the claimants to obtain an enforceable judgment against a solvent defendant (i.e. the parent company) warranted the joining of defendants in the Spanish courts.

Croatian private international law provides the option of suing two or more defendants in the capacity of 'co-litigants under substantive law' (Croatian *materijalni suparničari*, which corresponds to the German notion of *materielle Streitgenossenschaft*). The Croatian courts have jurisdiction to adjudicate the case against all defendants, provided one of those defendants has domicile or seat in Croatia. The notion of *materijalni suparničari* includes the situation in which their rights or obligations derive from the same factual and legal basis – *idem factum, idem ius* (the same contract or tortious act provides the basis for the claim and is subject to the same law).[87] This is essentially an assessment based on substantive law, in which the Croatian company law rules on piercing the corporate veil may play an important role.[88] It is possible not only to join a company and its director as co-defendants (because they are considered *materijalni suparničari*) before the same court,[89] but also a company and its shareholders.[90] Probably the most frequent case is where a company shareholder is held liable for the non-paid wages to the company employees.[91]

87 This term is defined in Art. 196(1)(1) of the Civil Procedure Act, Official Gazette of the Republic of Croatia 53/1991, 91/1992, 112/1999, 129/2000, 88/2001, 117/2003, 88/2005, 2/2007, 96/2008, 84/2008, 123/2008, 57/2011, 25/2013 and 89/2014.

88 The case law related to domestic situations is likewise applicable in cross-border ones, as the legal concepts on which jurisdiction is based (*materijalni suparničari*) is the same.

89 See, e.g., High Commercial Court of the Republic of Croatia, Pž-2775/03, 10.12.2002. Accessible at www.iusinfo.hr.

90 See, e.g., Supreme Court of the Republic of Croatia, Pž-6369/03, 17.2.2004. Accessible at www.vsrh.hr.

91 See, e.g., Supreme Court of the Republic of Croatia, Rev-58/00, 14.02.2001. Accessible at www.vsrh.hr; High Commercial Court of the Republic of Croatia, Pž-9140/03, 17.1.2006, *Informator*, Nos. 5572–5573, 1.8.2007.

The most publicized case involving the joining of a foreign subsidiary in litigation against an EU-domiciled parent company is currently pending in the Netherlands. According to Dutch private international law, a Dutch court may exercise jurisdiction over a foreign subsidiary when the claims against parent and subsidiary are so closely connected as to justify the joining of defendants for reasons of process efficiency.[92] In a 2010 interlocutory judgment, the District Court of The Hague accepted jurisdiction over Royal Dutch Shell Plc (domiciled in the Netherlands and the United Kingdom) and its Nigerian subsidiary, the Shell Petroleum Development Company of Nigeria Ltd (SPDC) in a tort litigation for human rights abuses caused by oil spills in the Nigerian Bodo community. Not only were the claims against both companies intertwined and had the same legal basis (tort of negligence under Nigerian law), but, moreover, it was foreseeable for SPDC that it might be summoned in the Netherlands in connection with its alleged liability for the oil spills. In January 2013, the District Court dismissed the claims against Royal Dutch Shell Plc and all but one claim against SPDC.[93] However, the court maintained that the mere possibility that the Dutch parent company could be held liable was sufficient to attract a foreign subsidiary to the Dutch jurisdiction. Furthermore, the court's jurisdiction over the foreign subsidiary is sustained even if the claims against the parent company eventually proved unfounded. Both Shell and the Nigerian plaintiffs appealed the judgment. In December 2015, the Court of Appeal reinstated all claims against the Dutch parent company and SPCD, and ordered Shell to disclose documents concerning the maintenance of its oil pipelines.[94] It is interesting to note that the Court of Appeal applied the *Painer* test in assessing whether the joining was unforeseeable for the defendant. It rejected Shell's arguments on the matter on the grounds that, amongst other reasons, the recent increase in litigation against parent companies made it foreseeable for Royal Dutch Shell that it would be named as a defendant in a case like this.[95]

Under English common law, courts can accept jurisdiction over non-EU defendants for a claim in tort, provided that jurisdiction has been established over another defendant under the Brussels I Regulation or the common law, and that the non-EU defendant can be considered a necessary or proper party

92 See Art. 7(1) of the Dutch Code of Civil Procedure.

93 District Court The Hague, *Oguru-Efanga v Shell*, ECLI:NL:RBSGR:2013:BY9850 (30 January 2013); *Dooh v Shell*, ECLI:NL:RBSGR:2013:BY9854 (30 January 2013); *Akpan v Shell*, ECLI:NL:RBSGR:2013:BY9854 (30 January 2013).

94 Court of Appeal The Hague, *Oguru-Efanga v Shell*, ECLI:NL:GHDHA:2015:3588 (17 December 2015); *Dooh v Shell*, ECLI:NL:GHDHA:2015:3586 (17 December 2015); *Akpan v Shell*, ECLI:NL:GHDHA:2015:3587 (17 December 2015). The question of Shell's liability for the oil spills has not been answered on appeal but will be subject to further litigation; see Gerechtshof Den Haag, 'Dutch courts have jurisdiction in case against Shell Nigeria oil spills' (18 December 2015). Accessible at https://www.rechtspraak.nl/Organisatie-en-contact/Organisatie/Gerechtshoven/Gerechtshof-Den-Haag/Nieuws/Paginas/Dutch-Courts-have-jurisdiction-in-case-against-Shell-Nigeria-oil-spills.aspx.

95 *Akpan v Shell*, ECLI:NL:GHDHA:2015:3587 (17 December 2015) para. 3.6.

to the claim.[96] As the rationale for assuming jurisdiction in such cases is that it is more convenient and economical to litigate a dispute against connected parties in one court, no further connection between the non-EU defendant and the English forum is required. In a recent litigation with the same subject matter as the Dutch Shell case involving 15,000 claimants from Nigeria's Bodo community, the proceedings were originally issued against the Anglo-Dutch parent company Royal Dutch Shell Plc and its Nigerian subsidiary SPDC.[97] Later on, SPDC submitted to the jurisdiction of the English court on the condition that the claimants stayed proceedings against the parent company. The court decided that SPDC could in principle be held liable for oil spills resulting from a failure to take all reasonable steps to protect its oil infrastructure in Nigeria.[98] In January 2015 a settlement was reached according to which Shell is to pay £55 million compensation and to clean up the affected areas.[99]

1.4.4 *Pursuing civil remedies through criminal jurisdiction*

The ECHR (as international human rights law more generally) imposes obligations on EU Member States to ensure effective civil as well as criminal remedies for corporate human rights abuses committed within their human rights jurisdiction. If human rights abuses committed by foreign subsidiaries or contractors of EU-based companies also constitute an (international) crime, it can be beneficial for claimants to attract the case to the jurisdiction of an EU Member State by initiating criminal proceedings there. Criminal jurisdiction is not regulated by EU law and therefore falls within the responsibility of the Member States. Using criminal cases to pursue civil remedies can be of advantage where a Member State's rules on criminal jurisdiction encompass cases of extraterritorial corporate human rights abuses that would not otherwise fall within the competence of national courts under that state's private international law. However, this opportunity is rarely used at present and can incur significant costs for the victims, especially if the legal support for the victims of crime does not extend to the civil proceedings.

In Spain, as in a number of other Member States, criminal courts are competent to adjudicate civil claims arising out of a criminal offence.[100] This enables the application of Spain's traditionally far-reaching rules on universal criminal jurisdiction to civil cases involving human rights abuses by 'multinational' companies, provided that the tort also constitutes an international crime. Statutory reforms in 2009 and 2014 have restricted the scope of universal criminal

96 Civil Procedure Rules (1998) SI 1998/3132, r. 6.37.

97 High Court (QU), *Bodo Community v Shell*, Claim No. HQ 11X01280.

98 *The Bodo Community and Others v The Shell Petroleum Development Company of Nigeria Limited* [2014] EWHC 1973 (TCC).

99 See further https://www.leighday.co.uk/News/2015/January-2015/Shell-agrees-55m-compensation-deal-for-Nigeria-Del.

100 See Arts 109ff. of the Spanish Criminal Code.

jurisdiction, yet Spanish courts are still competent to hear claims relating to genocide, crimes against humanity, and war crimes. While there are a number of well-publicized universal criminal jurisdiction cases in Spain, victims of human rights abuses have not yet made use of the possibility of pursuing civil remedies before Spanish criminal courts.

Croatia's rules on universal criminal jurisdiction are sufficiently broad to permit a criminal prosecution of companies committing a crime anywhere, without the need to show a strong connection to the Croatian forum. A condition is that the crime is either punishable under both Croatian law and the law of the foreign jurisdiction, or that Croatia must prosecute that crime pursuant to its obligations in international law. Croatian criminal courts may entertain civil disputes in the so-called adhesion proceedings. In a 2008 Amendment to the Criminal Procedure Act,[101] the scope of claims was broadened to include any claim available under civil law. It is not entirely clear whether this rule may be relied upon in all cross-border disputes even beyond the specific rules of universal jurisdiction, but there seems to be room for such an interpretation. This is of considerable importance given that Croatian criminal courts have used the Croatian Legal Persons Responsibility for Criminal Offences Act[102] to convict not only companies but also their shareholders of economic crimes, without reference to the company law institute of 'piercing' the corporate veil.[103] Thus far, criminal judges have been rather unwilling to decide about civil damages in criminal proceedings. This is partly due to the fact that judges are under constant pressure to reduce the length of proceedings, and that their performance is evaluated irrespective of whether they accept to adhere to a civil claim to the criminal case.[104]

In France, victims of human rights abuses that also constitute a crime can become a *partie civile* in criminal proceedings against the responsible companies. This enables victims to obtain civil remedies for damages directly related to the commission of the crime. In August 2011, it transpired that the French company *Amesys* (a subsidiary of the French *Groupe Bull*) had provided the Libyan government with a computer program ('Eagle') used for surveillance and mass interception of internet communications. In October 2011, the Human Rights

101 Official Gazette of the Republic of Croatia, 152/2008, 76/2009, 80/2011, 91/2012, 143/2012, 56/2013, 145/2013 and 152/2014.

102 Official Gazette of the Republic of Croatia, 151/2003, 110/2007, 45/2011 and 143/2012.

103 See, e.g., Supreme Court of the Republic of Croatia, I Kž 724/01–7, 3.8.2005; Supreme Court of the Republic of Croatia, I Kž 818/12–9, 27.11.2013; Supreme Court of the Republic of Croatia, I Kž 626/14–6, 201.1.2015; all accessible at www.iusinfo.hr.

104 See Metodologija izrade ocjene sudaca [Methodology for Evaluation of Judges]. Accessible at: http://www.dsv.pravosudje.hr/index.php/dsv/propisi/metodologija_izrade_ocjene_sudaca; and Okvirna mjerila za rad sudaca [Framework Criteria for the Performance of Judges]. Accessible at https://pravosudje.gov.hr/UserDocsImages/dokumenti/Pravo%20na%20pristup%20informacijama/Zakoni%20i%20ostali%20propisi/Okvirna%20mjerila%20za%20rad%20sudaca.pdf.

League and the International Federation of Human Rights (FIDH) filed a criminal complaint against *Amesys* before the Paris Court of First Instance, alleging that its software had enabled the Libyan government to commit serious human rights abuses including torture and inhuman and degrading treatment.[105] The Public Prosecutor initially declined to initiate criminal proceedings. The judge nevertheless ordered an investigation into the alleged complicity of *Amesys* in the human rights abuses committed by the Gaddafi regime. An appeal by the Office of the Public Prosecutor was unsuccessful. In January 2013, the Paris Court of Appeal directed the case to a judicial unit specializing in war crimes, crimes against humanity, and genocide.[106] In May 2013, five victims who had been arrested and tortured in Libya were admitted as '*parties civiles*' to the lawsuit, following which the judges ordered an assessment of the civil damages they had suffered.[107] The case is still pending.

1.5 Conclusions and recommendations

- When deciding on their jurisdiction in private litigation for human rights abuses by multinational companies, state courts of EU Member States must have due regard to their human rights obligations to ensure effective civil remedies under the ECHR and international human rights law.
- EU Member States should consider allowing their domestic courts to exercise jurisdiction over civil claims concerning business-related human rights abuses against subsidiaries, wherever they are based, of companies domiciled within their jurisdiction if such claims are closely connected with civil claims against the latter companies.
- EU Member States' courts should reverse the foreseeability test applied in the ECJ's *Painer* case for joining actions on different legal bases, in cases where parents and subsidiaries are joined together. This would put the burden on the defendant company to prove that it was unforeseeable that the parent may be held jointly liable with the subsidiary, rather than the plaintiffs having to argue that it was foreseeable.
- Where companies are not domiciled within their jurisdiction, EU Member States should consider, or not retreat from, the possibility of allowing their domestic courts to exercise jurisdiction over civil claims concerning business-related human rights abuses against such a business enterprise, if no other

105 P. Sonne and M. Coker, 'Firms Aided Libyan Spies: First Look Inside Security Unit Shows How Citizens Were Tracked', *Wall Street Journal* (30 August 2011). Accessible at http://online.wsj.com/articles/SB10001424053111904199404576538721260166388.

106 See FIDH, *Amesys case: The investigation chamber green lights the investigative proceedings on the sale of surveillance equipment by Amesys to the Gaddafi regime* (15 January 2013). Accessible at https://www.fidh.org/en/north-africa-middle-east/libya/Amesys-Case-The-Investigation-12752.

107 See FIDH, The Amesys case (20 September 2015). Accessible at https://www.fidh.org/IMG/pdf/report_amesys_case_eng.pdf.

effective forum guaranteeing a fair trial is available (*forum necessitatis*), and there is a sufficiently close connection to the Member State concerned.

- EU Member States should consider introducing a rebuttable presumption of control in determining a subsidiary's central administration; a wholly owned or majority-owned subsidiary is presumed to have its central administration with the parent company, unless the parent can prove that the subsidiary makes relevant business decisions independently from the parent and has no ties with the parent's place of incorporation.

2 Judicial remedies

The issue of applicable law

L.F.H. (Liesbeth) Enneking

2.1 Introduction

This chapter addresses the issue of applicable law, thus dealing with the question of under what circumstances the national rules of tort law of the EU Member States would be applied in cases brought before EU Member State courts against EU-based internationally operating business enterprises in relation to the harmful impacts of their activities – or those of their subsidiaries or business partners – on people and the planet in non-EU host countries. In addition, it also addresses some of the main practical and procedural barriers that host country victims of corporate human rights and environmental abuse may encounter when seeking to get access to remedy before EU Member State courts.

This chapter will start out with a general overview in section 2 of the legal context within which the issue of applicable law is set. The issue of applicable law is largely determined by EU law in the form of the Rome II Regulation, which will be discussed in section 3. The issue of practical and procedural circumstances is largely determined by the national rules of civil procedure of the country in which a particular case is brought. Although a full comparative study of relevant procedural rules in the different EU Member States falls outside of the scope of this report, section 4 will provide an indication of the main thresholds. At the end of each section, the findings will be discussed and put into the context of relevant provisions of the UN Guiding Principles (UNGPs). This chapter will close up with an overall conclusion in section 5.

2.2 Legal context

With an increasing number of liability cases being brought before EU Member State courts against EU-based companies in relation to the harmful impacts of their activities on people and the planet in non-EU host countries, the issue of access to justice before EU Member State courts in a business & human rights context has gained significance.

2.2.1 Foreign direct liability and beyond[1]

Over the past two decades, Western societies around the world have witnessed a growing trend towards transnational civil liability claims against internationally operating business enterprises in relation to harm caused to people and the planet in the course of their operations – or those of their subsidiaries or supply chain partners – in developing host countries. These so-called foreign direct liability cases are typically initiated by host country citizens who, often with the help of home country based NGOs, turn to courts in the Western society home countries of the internationally operating business enterprises involved in search of an adequate level of protection of their human rights, their health and safety, and their local environment.

In many of these cases, plaintiffs seek to hold accountable the Western society based parent companies of multinational corporations, often together with any local (sub-)subsidiaries that were in charge of carrying out the harmful operations in question. In more recent cases, claims have also been directed at, for instance, Western society based retailers in relation to the harmful consequences of the operations of foreign (sub-)contractors in their supply chains. Another key feature of these cases is that the claims put forward are generally not only aimed at securing financial compensation for harm suffered by past activities, like more garden-variety tort cases. Instead, they are often also, and sometimes especially, aimed at: first, trying to get the internationally operating business enterprises involved to exercise a higher level of care for the local inhabitants and local environment in their future operations in the host countries involved and to persuade their subsidiaries or supply chain partners into doing the same; second, trying to create transparency and debate in the Western society home countries of the internationally operating business enterprises involved with respect to the detrimental impacts that the operations of 'their' companies may have on people and the planet in developing host countries.

Up until now, the vast majority of these foreign direct liability cases have been brought before US federal courts on the basis of the Alien Tort Statute

1 This section is largely based on: Liesbeth F. H. Enneking et al., Zorgplichten van Nederlandse Ondernemingen inzake Internationaal Maatschappelijk Verantwoord Ondernemen, Report of a study commissioned by the Dutch Ministries of Security & Justice and Foreign Affairs, The Hague, Boom Juridische uitgevers, 2016, report (in Dutch) and executive summary (in English) accessible at https://www.wodc.nl/onderzoeksdatabase/2531-maatschappelijk-verantwoord-ondernemen-in-het-buitenland.aspx; Liesbeth F. H. Enneking, 'The Future of Foreign Direct Liability? Exploring the International Relevance of the Dutch Shell Nigeria Case' 1 *Utrecht Law Review* (2014) 44–54; Liesbeth F. H. Enneking, *Foreign Direct Liability and Beyond – Exploring the Role of Tort Law in Promoting International Corporate Social Responsibility and Accountability* (2012) Eleven International Publishing: The Hague.

(ATS).[2] This ancient US federal statute, which was 'rediscovered' in the 1980s by human rights activists, turned out to provide a legal basis for civil claims before US federal courts in relation to violations of public international law norms perpetrated around the world. It has been hailed by human rights activists as a much-needed accountability mechanism for human rights violations perpetrated in developing societies where victims' chances of obtaining (enforceable) remedies may be compromised by poorly functioning legal systems, corruption and/or favouritism.[3]

Initially, the ATS was mainly used as a basis for civil claims against individual perpetrators of international human rights violations or international crimes, like Karadzic and Marcos. From the mid-1990s onwards, however, it has also become a popular basis for civil liability claims against corporate actors in relation to their alleged involvement in human rights violations perpetrated in host countries.[4] The result of this development so far is that over 150 ATS-based foreign direct liability claims have been brought before the US federal courts against a wide range of multinationals with a basis or at least a presence in the US, for their alleged involvement in international human rights abuses perpetrated in countries such as Burma, South Africa, Ecuador, Nigeria, and Sudan.[5] High-profile examples include claims against a large group of multinationals including General Motors, IBM and DaimlerChrysler for their alleged involvement in the human rights violations perpetrated by the South African Apartheid regime, and the claims against oil multinational Shell for its alleged involvement in the human rights violations perpetrated by the Nigerian military regime against environmental activists in the Ogoniland region of the Niger Delta in the mid-1990s.[6]

But foreign direct liability cases have also, and increasingly so, been brought before US state courts and before courts in other Western societies like Canada, the UK, Sweden, Italy, and the Netherlands. In the absence of an ATS equivalent outside the US (federal) legal system, these claims are often based on general principles of tort law and the tort of negligence in particular. As a consequence, the claims in these non-ATS-based foreign direct liability

2 28 United States Code §1350. This statute, which has famously been referred to as a 'legal Lohengrin', since 'no one seems to know whence it came' (*IIT v Vencap, Ltd.*, 519 F.2d 1001 (2nd Cir. 1975) (Friendly, J., at 1015)) – or, more particularly: what exactly the 1789 framers had in mind when they enacted it – provides: 'The district courts shall have original jurisdiction of any civil action by an alien for a tort only, committed in violation of the law of nations or a treaty of the United States'.

3 See in more detail, for example, Enneking 2012, *op. cit.*, pp. 77–87, 277–278.

4 *Ibid.*, pp. 77–83.

5 See, for instance, Jonathan C. Drimmer and Sarah R. Lamoree, 'Think Globally, Sue Locally: Trends and Out-of-Court Tactics in Transitional Tort Actions', 2 *Berkeley Journal of International Law* (2011) 456–527, 465.

6 See in more detail and with further references: business-humanrights.org/en/apartheid-reparations-lawsuits-re-so-africa and https://business-humanrights.org/en/shell-lawsuit-re-nigeria-kiobel-wiwa, respectively.

cases tend to revolve not primarily around alleged violations of international (human rights) norms, but more often around alleged violations of non-written norms pertaining to proper societal conduct and due care with respect to health and safety, labour standards and the environment. In countries such as Belgium, France and Switzerland, similar cases have presented themselves in the form of criminal proceedings initiated at the instigation of victims and NGOs.[7]

A 2015 comparative study on the duties of care of Dutch companies in the field of international corporate social responsibility revealed that, since the early 1990s, at least 35 foreign direct liability cases have been pursued before courts in the six countries investigated (Belgium, France, Germany, the Netherlands, the UK, and Switzerland).[8] Similar cases have been reported in a number of other countries that fell outside the scope of this study including, for instance Sweden,[9] which means that the number of these cases pursued so far before EU Member State courts is likely to be around 40 in total.

Well known examples include the civil claims that were brought before the High Court of Justice in London by a large group of Ivorian citizens following the Probo Koala toxic waste dumping incident,[10] and the claims against Shell by Nigerian farmers and the Dutch NGO Milieudefensie in relation to damage caused by oil spills in the Ogoniland region of the Niger Delta that are currently pending before the Hague Court of Appeals.[11] It should be noted that of these 35 cases, only three have resulted in a final judicial decision on the merits in which the defendant companies were held liable. Many of the other cases have either been dismissed at an early stage of the proceedings, often due to lack of jurisdiction or lack of sufficient evidence substantiating the claims, or settled out of court (see Figure 2.1).

These foreign direct liability cases play a crucial role in exploring the hard law edges of international soft law instruments like the UN Policy Framework on Business and Human Rights and the accompanying UNGPs.[12]

Their significance flows from the fact that we are living in a globalizing world in which the production processes of corporate actors are increasingly becoming transnational affairs, but where adequate regulatory mechanisms to deal with

7 See in more detail, for example: Enneking *et al.* 2016, *op. cit.* pp. 23–29 *et seq.*; Enneking 2012, *op. cit.* pp. 87–91.

8 Enneking *et al.* 2016, *op. cit.* pp. 35–44, 163–164, 190–193, 224–231, 265–275, 315–316, 439–442.

9 See, in more detail on the Swedish case: Rasmus Klocker Larsen, 'Foreign direct liability claims in Sweden: Learning from "Arica Victims KB" v "Boliden Mineral AB"?', 4 *Nordic Journal of International Law* (2014) 404–438.

10 See in more detail and with further references: https://business-humanrights.org/en/trafigura-lawsuits-re-côte-d'ivoire.

11 See in more detail and with further references: https://business-humanrights.org/en/shell-lawsuit-re-oil-pollution-in-nigeria.

12 See in more detail: Enneking *et al.* 2016, *op. cit.* pp. 23–24, 427–432, 450–453.

Country	Corporate Law	Civil Law	Outcomes	Criminal Law	Outcomes	Totals
Belgium	0	0	n/a	1	• 1 dismissed	1
Germany	0	3	• 1 out-of-court settlement • 2 ongoing	2	• 1 status unclear • 1 prosecutor ends investigation	5
France	0	2	• 1 compensation granted • 1 dismissed	8	• 1 status unclear • 1 prosecutor ends investigation • 1 prosecutor ends investigation, claim settled out of court • 3 ongoing • 2 ongoing with joint civil claim	10
UK	0	13	• 6 out-of-court settlements • 1 partly settled, partly ongoing • 2 dismissed • 4 ongoing	0	n/a	13
Switzerland	0	0	n/a	2	• 2 prosecutor ends investigation	2
Netherlands	0	2	• 1 compensation granted (partly) • 1 partly dismissed, partly ongoing	2	• 1 conviction • 1 dropped	4
Totals	0	20		15		35

Figure 2.1 Overview of relevant cases[1]

[1] Derived from: Enneking *et al.* 2016, *op. cit.* p. 440.

these internationally operating business enterprises and the impacts of their worldwide activities are lacking. In a world with an international legal order that is still premised on the traditional idea of sovereign nation states, domestic public law regulations in principle remain territorially confined. At the same time, international treaties are few and far between and are usually either confined to a very specific subject matter, or broad but vague. And although soft law instruments and self-regulatory mechanisms such as corporate codes of conduct may strike a chord with corporate leaders in the field of international corporate social responsibility, they are less well suited to deal with corporate laggards in this context due to the lack of a mandatory nature and/or adequate enforcement.

This leaves the field of private law, and that of tort law in particular, as an important mechanism to ensure that internationally operating business enterprises take seriously their responsibility to minimize the risk that the activities they undertake in the pursuit of profits will detrimentally affect people and planet elsewhere. One of the big advantages of relying on private law mechanisms in this context is that potential concerns by the states involved over extraterritorial infringements of one another's sovereignty are dealt with through the field of private international law. However, the role that national systems of tort law may play in promoting socially responsible behaviour by internationally operating business enterprises and business respect for human rights is, in the end, strongly dependent on the feasibility for the victims of irresponsible business practices of successfully pursuing foreign direct liability claims.[13]

An analysis of the claims pursued so far shows that the feasibility of these cases is determined by four main factors: 1) whether the home country court seized of the matter has jurisdiction to hear the claim; 2) which national system of tort law the court will apply in determining the validity of the claim; 3) what the conditions for liability are that are connected to the legal basis on which the claim is brought; 4) to what extent the procedural rules and practical circumstances in the forum country are conducive to the pursuit of this type of litigation.[14] This report will address the issue of applicable law as well as that of practical and procedural circumstances in the forum country. In doing so, its focus is on foreign direct liability cases pursued on the basis of tort law. A further discussion of the feasibility, applicable law, and practical and procedural circumstances in cases pursued on the basis of the criminal law falls outside the scope of this report – and of this project.

2.2.2 *Private international law and extraterritoriality*[15]

As has been mentioned, the point of departure in today's international legal order of sovereign nation states remains that each state, in principle, has the supreme authority to prescribe and enforce rules and regulations with respect to actors and activities within its territory. However, as a result of growing global interconnectedness, actors and activities are increasingly situated in

13 See in more detail: Enneking 2012, *op. cit.* pp. 443–521.
14 *Ibid.*, pp. 129–203.
15 This section is derived from: Enneking 2012, *op. cit.* pp. 137–140.

transnational rather than domestic contexts and are thus potentially subject to the authority of more than one state. The resulting competing claims to regulatory authority by different states with respect to those actors and activities raise questions of international jurisdiction. These questions may be subdivided into questions of: adjudicative jurisdiction (referring to a state's authority to have its courts adjudicate on disputes and render judgments in an international context); prescriptive jurisdiction (referring to a state's authority to apply its laws in an international context); and enforcement jurisdiction (referring to a state's authority to enforce compliance with its laws in an international context).[16]

In line with the idea that the contemporary international legal order is made up of different sovereign nation states each with exclusive authority over actors and activities within their territories, the jurisdiction of states to exercise any of these types of international jurisdiction over actors and activities outside their territory (extraterritorially) is limited. In theory, these limitations are defined either by the field of public international law where public law rights and obligations are concerned, or by the field of private international law where private law rights and obligations are concerned. These two fields of law are of a very different nature. Whereas the former justifies international jurisdiction in spatial terms with a strong focus on territoriality and state sovereignty, the latter focuses on connecting factors between the private actors and activities in question and the different states involved.

Furthermore, the field of public international law revolves around state interests and as such tends to be highly politicized, while the traditional and still popular basic assumption in the field of private international law, in Europe at least, is that this field of law is apolitical, due also to the fact that the domestic systems of private law that it is concerned with are assumed to be relatively free of state intervention and insulated from public interests. According to Michaels, this traditional view can be traced back to Von Savigny's conception that private law is apolitical and should as such be sharply distinguished from the field of public law. He argues that this traditional conception of private international law as an essentially value-neutral, apolitical field of law as originally developed by Von Savigny cannot adequately deal with the contemporary challenges of globalization.[17]

In practice, the two fields are also closely interconnected. The more blurred the boundary between public law and private law becomes, for instance where

16 See in more detail, for instance: Jennifer A. Zerk, *Extraterritorial Jurisdiction: Lessons for the Business and Human Rights Sphere from Six Regulatory Areas*, A report for the Harvard Corporate Social Responsibility Initiative to help inform the mandate of the UNSG's Special Representative on Business and Human Rights, 2009, accessible at https://www.hks.harvard.edu/m-rcbg/CSRI/publications/workingpaper_59_zerk.pdf; Gary P. Born and Peter B. Rutledge *International Civil Litigation in United States Courts*, (2007) Wolters Kluwer Law & Business: Austin, TX, (4th ed.) 1–217.

17 R. Michaels, *Globalizing Savigny? The State in Savigny's Private International Law and the Challenge of Europeanization and Globalization*, Duke Law School Faculty Scholarship Series, no. 15, 2005. Accessible at http://ssrn.com/abstract=796228.

private law and civil disputes are given a more 'public' character because they are applied by the government and/or by private actors themselves to enforce public laws, promote public policies, protect public interests or facilitate societal change more generally, the more principles of public and private international law come together.[18] Thus, the question may be raised of whether (the issues sought to be resolved through) the field of private international law may not under certain circumstances be rather 'public' in both character and consequences. Symeonides argues in this respect that

> the word 'private', which echoes the private-public law distinction prevalent in Europe, assumes that the cases that fall within the scope of this subject are garden-variety private-law disputes that implicate only the interests of the litigants and not the interests of the states having contacts with the case. If this were true, these cases would not differ from intra-state cases which are always governed by forum law. Precisely because of their multistate dimension, conflicts cases implicate the laws of more than one state, which may embody different objectives, values, or policies. Although these states are not the actual disputants as they would be in a public international law dispute, it is unrealistic to assume that they are wholly indifferent to the way these conflicts cases are resolved.[19]

In fact, the idea of the field of private international law as an apolitical, neutral field of law that does not involve state interests has long been abandoned in the US, in favour of an approach that recognizes that the conflicting interests involved in this field go far beyond the interests of the parties directly involved in a transnational private law dispute and concern also societal, public and ultimately state interests.[20] Meanwhile, also in Europe there is a growing awareness of and sensitivity to the broader, more public implications of the role of private international law in transnational private law disputes, even though the consideration of these implications remains much less overt than in the US.[21]

With respect to the future role of public interests in the field of private international law, Symeonides predicts:

> As we proceed down the path of the twenty-first century, we can expect that states will, even more boldly, assert their interest in multistate private-law disputes.[22]

18 Similarly, J. A. Zerk, *Multinationals and Corporate Social Responsibility* (2006), Cambridge University Press: Cambridge, 104–142.

19 S. C. Symeonides, 'The American Revolution and the European Evolution in Choice of Law: Reciprocal Lessons', 5 *Tulane Law Review* (2008) 1741–1799 (hereinafter: Symeonides 2008a).

20 See, in more detail: Symeonides 2008a, *op. cit.* pp. 1784–1794.

21 *Ibid.*

22 *Ibid.*, p. 1794.

The resulting confluence of public and private international law may result in complex issues that challenge existing paradigms in both fields of law.[23] An example is the growing reliance on civil procedures before domestic courts to address international crimes such as genocide, crimes against humanity, war crimes, torture, slavery, and terrorism. This tendency has the potential of causing conflict with (the harmonization of) domestic civil procedural rules, and raises questions with respect to the lawful exercise of universal (civil) jurisdiction where the domestic legal order in which the claim is brought has little or no connections to the actors or activities in question.[24]

Dubinsky argues in this respect:

> In attempting to adjudicate claims arising out of severe and systematic human rights abuses, domestic courts are trying to fill an enforcement gap, a task for which they were not designed.[25]

He suggests that in order to tackle these issues, a set of common principles of procedural law (including private international law) should be developed that would be applicable to the adjudication of civil claims pertaining to grave human rights violations, no matter where those claims would be brought.[26]

Foreign direct liability cases, due to their transnationality and distinct public interest nature, are a clear example of cases that lie at the plane of intersection between both areas of law. Accordingly, despite the fact that these cases are essentially concerned with private law disputes over the private interrelationships between the host country plaintiffs and the defendant companies, they also tend to raise issues of international adjudicatory and prescriptive jurisdiction and extraterritoriality. After all, home country courts are typically asked in these cases to exercise authority over actors and activities that predominantly lie outside the territorial ambit of those home countries, by exercising jurisdiction over foreign direct liability claims and by, where possible, determining them on the basis of home country tort standards. This may be controversial where this is perceived by the host countries involved as an 'interference in their sovereign rights to regulate corporations within their own borders, and to pursue their own economic, social and cultural interests'.[27]

23 For a more detailed discussion, see A. Mills, *The Confluence of Public and Private International Law* (2009) Cambridge: Cambridge University Press.

24 For a more detailed discussion, see P. R. Dubinsky, 'Human Rights Law Meets Private Law Harmonization: The Coming Conflict', 1 *Yale Journal of International Law* (2005) 211–318.

25 *Ibid.*, p. 302.

26 *Ibid.*, pp. 312–317.

27 D. Augenstein (2010) *Study of the Legal Framework on Human Rights and the Environment Applicable to European Enterprises Operating outside the European Union*, Report of a study prepared for the European Commission by the University of Edinburgh. Accessible at http://en.frankbold.org/sites/default/files/tema/101025_ec_study_final_report_en_0.pdf. In fact, issues of extraterritoriality have been raised in various foreign direct liability

This means that even though the exercise of jurisdiction by home country courts over foreign direct liability claims or the adjudication of those claims on the basis of home country tort principles may be firmly based on applicable rules of private international law, issues of extraterritoriality may remain. Zerk has noted in this context that

> [s]uperficially, a court may only be deciding a dispute between private parties. In reality, though, judicial approaches to problems posed by multinationals in the private law sphere will reflect a set of principles and assumptions, conscious or unconscious, about the appropriate distribution of risk, reward and responsibilities between the different actors involved. But, as well as having a regulatory context, case law on matters of private international law also has regulatory consequences to the extent that it affects the balance of risks and rewards against which the investment decisions of multinationals are subsequently made. In this sense, even the act of deferring to the courts of another state, for whatever reason, is a 'regulatory' act.[28]

Accordingly, underlying issues of sovereignty and extraterritoriality play a prominent role in providing the socio-political context of foreign direct liability cases and the background to private international law-related issues such as the determination of the applicable law in these cases.

2.2.3 *Discussion*

One of the main focal points of the debates in the EU Member States on access to judicial remedy for victims of corporate human rights abuses is the contemporary trend towards foreign direct liability cases: transnational (civil) liability claims against internationally operating business enterprises in relation to harm caused to people and the planet in the course of their operations – or those of their subsidiaries or supply chain partners – in developing host countries. Over the past two decades, the prevalence of this type of litigation before EU Member State courts has strongly increased, from a mere handful of cases in the 1990s to a total of around 40 cases pursued in various EU Member States up until now – and counting.

The significance of these cases lies in the role they may play in promoting international corporate social responsibility and in fostering corporate respect for human rights, as set out in the UNGPs, while at the same time providing a potential redress mechanism for victims of corporate environmental or human

---

cases, including for instance the Bhopal litigation (*In re Union Carbide gas plant disaster at Bhopal, India in December 1984*, 634 F.Supp. 842 (SDNY 1986), p. 862–867) and the Apartheid litigation (*In re South African Apartheid Litigation*, 617 F.Supp.2d 228 (SDNY 2009), p. 276–286).

28 Zerk 2006, *op. cit.* p. 114.

rights abuse. They typically originate in developing host countries where legal standards relating to the protection of human rights, the environment, health and safety, and labour circumstances are not very strict or not very strictly enforced. These cases make it possible for individuals and communities who have suffered harm as a result of the activities of internationally operating business enterprises in these host countries to turn to courts in the Western society home countries of those business enterprises in order to obtain a more adequate level of protection of their people and planet related interests.[29]

What plays an important role in these cases is that legal procedures before local host country courts are often problematic, regardless of the merits of the claims involved. Reasons for this may be for instance that the local judiciary is not independent, that there is a fear of persecution, that the individuals or communities involved face discrimination, that the host country legal system is not equipped to effectively deal with complex legal claims, that it would be difficult to locally enforce a court verdict, etc. This means that getting access to judicial remedies before home country courts is often crucial for the victims' chances of addressing and obtaining redress for infringements of their environmental and human rights interests as a result of activities carried out by or for EU-based internationally operating business enterprises in the host countries involved.[30]

Whether these foreign direct liability cases can play a role in providing victims of corporate human rights and environmental abuse with access to judicial remedies before EU Member State courts is dependent on a number of factors that determine the feasibility of these cases. These include, *inter alia*, what law is to be applied in determining the validity of the claims, and whether there are barriers inherent in the procedural rules and practical circumstances in the EU Member States that may prevent these cases from being pursued, regardless of their merits.[31] This report focuses on the second and the fourth of these factors; the first is dealt with in the report on jurisdiction, while the third is (partly) dealt with in the report on standards of care.

2.3 Applicable law[32]

Once it has been established that the court before which a foreign direct liability claim has been brought has jurisdiction to hear the matter, the question arises

29 Enneking *et al.* 2016, *op. cit.* pp. 27–28; Enneking 2012, *op. cit.* pp. 107–117.

30 *Ibid.*

31 Enneking *et al.* 2016, *op. cit.* pp. 27–28; Enneking 2012, *op. cit.* pp. 132–137.

32 This section is largely derived from: Enneking 2012. See also L.F.H. Enneking,' The Common Denominator of the Trafigura Case, Foreign Direct Liability Cases and the Rome II Regulation', 2 *European Review of Private Law* (2008) 283–311.

on the basis of which legal norms the transboundary civil claim should be adjudicated. After all, transnational litigation inevitably presents questions of applicable law (or conflict-of-law) where two or more states are able to prescribe substantive rules of conduct regulating the private actors and activities in dispute. Accordingly, courts dealing with transnational civil disputes need to select, on the basis of the domestic rules of private international law that apply in the forum country, which of the legal systems of the states connected to the transnational civil dispute should govern the claims. Rules of private international law may also flow from non-domestic sources of law, such as the EU's many regulations on the law applicable to civil disputes in various subject matter areas.

In principle, different conflict-of-law regimes may apply depending on the characterization of the transnational claims in dispute as tort claims, contractual claims, or otherwise. In this report, the focus will be on applicable law issues in foreign direct liability cases pursued on the basis of tort law. Due to these cases' strong connections to the host country (since they typically pertain to harm caused to people and planet in the host country as a result of activities carried out there), it is not at all a given that the home country courts adjudicating foreign direct liability claims will be able to do so on the basis of home country substantive norms on tort law. In fact, in many of these cases the home country courts involved will have to formulate their judgment with respect to the alleged wrongfulness of the corporate conduct in question – as well as with respect to its legal consequences – on the basis of foreign (often host country) rules of tort law.

2.3.1 Rome II Regulation: general rule

In foreign direct liability cases brought before courts of the EU Member States, the issue of applicable law is largely determined by EU law in the form of the Rome II Regulation.[33] This regulation provides a mandatory and exhaustive regime of unified rules on applicable law in cases of non-contractual liability (hereinafter, tort) involving events giving rise to damage that have occurred on or after 11 January 2009.[34] Pursuant to its principal aim of realizing uniformity

33 Regulation (EC) No 864/2007 of the European Parliament and of the Council of 11 July 2007 on the law applicable to non-contractual obligations (Rome II), *OJEU* L199/40 (31 July 2007). Note that the Regulation covers torts occurring within and outside the EU alike and may as such also lead to the application of the law of a non-EU Member State; it's geographical scope is universal (Art. 3 Rome II Regulation).

34 Tort claims brought before EU Member State courts after 11 January 2009, but pertaining to events giving rise to damage that occurred before 11 January 2009, fall outside the temporal scope of the Rome II Regulation and are governed by the domestic rules on applicable law in tort cases of the forum country; the same is true for tort claims that have been initiated before 11 January 2009. See ECJ Case C-412/10, 6 September 2011, [2011] ECR I-11603 (*Homawoo v GMF*). A further discussion of domestic rules on applicable law in tort cases in the various EU Member States falls outside the scope of this report. See, for a brief discussion of relevant Dutch rules, for instance, Enneking 2012, *op. cit.* pp. 223–224.

in the choice of law decisions by the courts of the EU Member States,[35] the Regulation provides a relatively neutral 'system of tightly written black-letter rules with relatively few escapes and little room for judicial discretion' that is focused on jurisdiction-selection (conflicts justice) rather than content-oriented law selection (material justice).[36]

The Rome II Regulation takes as its point of departure the applicability of the *lex loci damni*, a specification of the traditional *lex loci delicti* rule. Consequently, it is the law of the country in which the damage occurs that in principle applies under the Regulation, 'irrespective of the country in which the event giving rise to the damage occurred and irrespective of the country or countries in which the indirect consequences of that event occur'.[37] On the basis of this general rule, it is the tort law of the host country that will in principle be applicable in foreign direct liability cases that are brought before EU Member State courts. This rule in principle also applies if the tort in question is a transboundary tort, in the sense that the act (or omission) giving rise to the damage is located in one country (the *Handlungsort*) whereas the harm resulting from that act (or omission) is located in another country (the *Erfolgsort*).[38]

There are a number of matters that in particular fall within the scope of the law that is applicable on the basis the Rome II Regulation's rules. These include:

> a) the basis and the extent of liability, including the determination of persons who may be held liable for acts performed by them; b) the grounds for exemption from liability, any limitation of liability and any division of liability;

35 See recital 6 Rome II Regulation: 'The proper functioning of the internal market creates a need, in order to improve the predictability of the outcome of litigation, certainty as to the law applicable and the free movement of judgments, for the conflict-of-law rules in the Member States to designate the same national law irrespective of the country of the court in which an action is brought'.

36 See, for a critical appraisal S. C. Symeonides, 'Rome II and Tort Conflicts: A Missed Opportunity', 1 *American Journal of Comparative Law* (2008) 173–222, 178–186) (Symeonides 2008b).

37 Art. 4(1) Rome II Regulation. According to the Explanatory Memorandum to the Commission's proposal for the Rome II Regulation, this choice for the *lex loci damni* as the Regulation's starting point is justified by the concern for certainty in the law, as well as by the consideration that 'the modern concept of the law of civil liability [. . .] is no longer [. . .] oriented towards punishing for fault-based conduct: nowadays, it is the compensation function that dominates' (COM(2003) 427, p. 12). It is further asserted that this rule 'strikes a fair balance between the interests of the person claimed to be liable and the person sustaining the damage, and also reflects the modern approach to civil liability and the development of systems of strict liability' (Recital 16 Rome II Regulation). See, critically, Symeonides 2008b, *op. cit.* pp. 186–192, and (with a focus on foreign direct liability cases) Enneking 2008, *op. cit.* pp. 309–310.

38 Art. 4(1) Rome II Regulation. The classic example of a transboundary tort case is the Mines de Potasse case, which concerned the pollution of the river Rhine by chlorides from French potassium miners, causing environmental harm to Dutch farmers located downstream from their operations. ECJ Case C-21/76, 30 November 1976, [1976] ECR 01735 (*Bier/ Mines de Potasse d'Alsace*).

c) the existence, the nature and the assessment of damage or the remedy claimed; d) within the limits of powers conferred on the court by its procedural law, the measures which a court may take to prevent or terminate injury or damage or to ensure the provision of compensation; e) the question whether a right to claim damages or a remedy may be transferred, including by inheritance; f) persons entitled to compensation for damage sustained personally; g) liability for the acts of another person; h) the manner in which an obligation may be extinguished and rules of prescription and limitation, including rules relating to the commencement, interruption and suspension of a period of prescription or limitation.[39]

In addition, where the law that is applicable to a claim under the Rome II Regulation 'contains rules which raise presumptions of law or determine the burden of proof', those will also be applicable.[40]

There are two general escape clauses that accompany the Rome II Regulation's general rule of applicability of the *lex loci damni.*

The first pertains to the situation that the person claimed to be liable and the person sustaining damage both have their habitual residence in the same country at the time when the damage occurs.[41] In such a situation, the law of the country of the joint habitual residence shall be applied to the case. However, this situation is unlikely to arise in foreign direct liability claims that are brought by host country victims against Western society-based internationally operating business enterprises.[42] It may in theory play a role in claims that would be brought by these victims before EU Member State courts against (only) host country-based companies, but in such cases, leaving aside the question whether the court would have jurisdiction to hear the claim,[43] this rule would not lead to a different outcome (i.e. applicability of host country tort law).

The second pertains to the situation that 'it is clear from all the circumstances of the case that the tort/delict is manifestly more closely connected' with a country other than the one in which the damage has arisen and other than the one in which (if relevant) the parties have their joint habitual residence.[44] In such a situation, the law of this other country shall be applied to the case. Whether it would be possible in foreign direct liability cases to successfully argue that such a closer connection to another country – notably the EU Member State that is the home country of the corporate defendant involved – exists is unclear, however. The example of such a 'manifestly closer relationship' that is provided by the Regulation itself, 'a pre-existing relationship between the parties,

39 Art. 15 Rome II Regulation.
40 Art. 20(1) Rome II Regulation.
41 Art. 4(2) Rome II Regulation.
42 Similarly, G. Van Calster, *European Private International Law* (2013) Hart Publishing: Oxford, 439.
43 See in more detail on this matter the report on Jurisdiction.
44 Art. 4(3) Rome II Regulation.

such as a contract, that is closely connected with the tort/delict in question',[45] is unlikely to play a role in foreign direct liability cases.[46] Especially considering the fact that, in line with the Regulation's general aim of providing for certainty as to the applicable law and predictability concerning the outcome of litigation, this provision will have to be interpreted and applied restrictively.[47]

In addition, the Rome II Regulation leaves open the possibility that the parties to a foreign direct liability case that is brought before an EU Member State court jointly designate the law that is to be applied to the claims on the basis of an agreement entered into after the event giving rise to the damage occurred.[48] In reality, the chances that parties to a foreign direct liability case will agree on the law that is to be applied to the case seem slim, especially in those cases where circumstances such as the level of protection of the victims and the level of damages will vary widely according to the law that is applied to the case, as will often be the case in this context. At the same time, to the corporate defendants involved the application of foreign (host country) tort law by these courts may carry with it the additional benefit that any judgment on the issue of liability in favour of the plaintiffs would not create binding and/or useful precedent under the tort law of the EU Member State where they are based.

2.3.2 Rome II Regulation: special rule on environmental damage

Furthermore, the Regulation contains a number of special provisions for specific types of torts that deviate from the general rule of *lex loci damni*. Of these provisions, the special rule on environmental damages is likely to be especially relevant in the context of foreign direct liability cases.[49] On the basis of this rule, the tort victim in a transboundary tort case that arises out of environmental damage or damage sustained by persons or property as a result of such damage, is presented with the option of choosing the applicability of the law of the *Handlungsort* (*lex loci actus*) instead of that of the *Erfolgsort* (*lex loci damni*).[50] According to the Regulation, environmental damage in this sense should be understood as meaning

> adverse change in a natural resource, such as water, land or air, impairment of a function performed by that resource for the benefit of another natural

45 *Ibid.*

46 Similarly, Van Calster 2013, *op. cit.* p. 240; Enneking 2008, *op. cit.* p. 307.

47 Similarly, but in more detail, Peter Huber (ed.), *Rome II Regulation: Pocket Commentary* (2011) European Law Publishers: Munich, Sellier, 99–104; Enneking 2008, *op. cit.* pp. 300–302.

48 Art. 14 (1) (a) Rome II Regulation.

49 This special rule is not subject to either the common domicile exception (Art. 4(2)) or to the closer connection exception (Art. 4(3)); it does, however, leave open the possibility of a choice of law on the basis of Art. 14. See Huber 2011, *op. cit.* pp. 202–203, 214.

50 Art. 7 Rome II Regulation.

> resource or the public, or impairment of the variability among living organisms.[51]

In contrast to the Rome II Regulation's overall tendency towards policy neutrality, the special rule on environmental damage has been inspired by objectives of environmental protection policy, in combination with the concern that 'the exclusive connection to the place where the damage is sustained would also mean that a victim in a low-protection country would not enjoy the higher level of protection available in neighbouring countries'.[52] In its original proposal for the Regulation, the Commission justified the inclusion of this special rule on environmental damage as follows:

> Considering the Union's more general objectives in environmental matters, the point is not only to respect the victim's legitimate interests but also to establish a legislative policy that contributes to raising the general level of environmental protection, especially as the author of the environmental damage, unlike other torts or delicts, generally derives an economic benefit from his harmful activity. Applying exclusively the law of the place where the damage is sustained could give an operator an incentive to establish his facilities at the border so as to discharge toxic substances into a river and enjoy the benefit of the neighbouring country's laxer rules. This solution would be contrary to the underlying philosophy of the European substantive law of the environment and the "polluter pays" principle.[53]

This particular rule may be of significance for future foreign direct liability cases, at least those that involve environmental damage as specified in the Regulation, provided they can be constructed as transboundary tort claims in which the event giving rise to the damage in the host country has taken place in the home country of the corporate defendant. This may be the case for instance if a claim can be made that the home country-based parent company or retailer took decisions, made demands or implemented policies that eventually resulted in the environmental damage being caused in the host country, or failed to exercise adequate supervision over the host country activities where it could and should have done so.[54] It has been suggested that such an interpretation is in line with the notion of operator responsibility and the accompanying definition of operator in the EU Environmental Liability Directive.[55]

51 Recital 24 Rome II Regulation.
52 Explanatory Memorandum, *op. cit.* p. 19.
53 *Ibid.*, pp. 19–20.
54 Similarly: Enneking 2008, *op. cit.* pp. 212–218, 304–307.
55 Carmen Otera García-Castrillón, 'International Litigation Trends in Environmental Liability: A European Union – United States Comparative Perspective', 3 *Journal of Private International Law* (2011) 551–581, 571–572). See also Van Calster 2013, *op. cit.* pp. 173–174.

In these situations, the special rule on environmental damage would give the host country victims the option of choosing application of home country tort law, which may involve more relevant precedents, higher regulatory standards, stricter liabilities, more liberal rules on presumptions of law or on shifting the burden of proof, higher damages awards, etc. However, the question has been raised as to whether the environmental damage rule would indeed be applicable to these particular types of claims, or whether its scope is limited to more 'classic' cases of transboundary environmental damage such as may arise for instance from river pollution or an explosion at a chemical factory.[56] The real issue here seems to be whether this rule pertains only to situations of local conduct that result in transboundary environmental damage which is felt in a neighbouring country, or also to situations of transboundary conduct that results in local environmental damage in some far away (non-EU) country. Or, put in another way: do non-EU environmental interests also fall within the scope of Rome II's environmental policies?

Although the Commission proposal does indeed speak of 'neighbouring countries', there is nothing in the text of the provision itself that supports this narrow interpretation. In fact, such a narrow interpretation does not seem to be in line with the Rome II Regulation's universal application, nor with the environmental damage rule's main aim, which is to raise the overall level of environmental protection and of making the polluter pay.[57] As is stated in the Regulation itself:

> Regarding environmental damage, Article 174 of the Treaty, which provides that there should be a high level of protection based on the precautionary principle and the principle that preventive action should be taken, the principle of priority for corrective action at source and the principle that the polluter pays, fully justifies the use of the principle of discriminating in favour of the person sustaining the damage.[58]

In the end, the choice provided to environmental tort victims by Art. 7 for the law of the *Handlungsort* rather than the *Erfolgsort* is not meant to benefit the victims as such, but to

> promote the interests of the respective countries and of the Union as a whole in deterring pollution. Applying whichever of the two laws subjects

56 See, for instance, A. G. Castermans and J. A. Van Der Weide, *The Legal Liability of Dutch Parent Companies for Subsidiaries' Involvement in Violations of Fundamental, Internationally Recognised Rights'*, Report of a study prepared for the Dutch Ministries of Economic Affairs and Foreign Affairs, 15 December 2009. Accessible at http://ssrn.com/abstract=1626225, p. 53.

57 See Arts 3 and 7 Rome II Regulation and Explanatory Memorandum, *op. cit.* pp. 9–10, 19–20.

58 Recital 25 Rome II Regulation.

> the polluter to a higher standard promotes this interest. Giving the victim a choice is simply the vehicle for ensuring this result.[59]

Whether and how the special rule on environmental damage may play a role in future foreign direct liability cases is a question that may eventually have to be answered by the ECJ, which has yet to render a decision on the interpretation and the scope of application of this rule.

2.3.3 Rome II Regulation: relevant exceptions

Apart from those cases that may be brought under the special rule for environmental damage, the Rome II Regulation's general rule of *lex loci damni* will in most cases result in the applicability of host country tort law in foreign direct liability cases. Nonetheless, there are a number of ways in which home country legal rules and standards that are relevant to the issue in dispute may find application even in foreign direct liability cases that are decided on the basis of host country rules of tort law.

2.3.3.1 Overriding mandatory provisions

First of all, there is the possibility under the Rome II Regulation for the EU Member State court seized of a matter to apply so-called overriding mandatory provisions (or, public order legislation, *règles d'application immédiate*) of the law of the forum that are relevant to the subject matter in dispute, irrespective of the law that governs the claim.[60] According to the ECJ, overriding mandatory provisions can be defined as

> national provisions compliance with which has been deemed to be so crucial for the protection of the political, social or economic order in the Member State concerned as to require compliance therewith by all persons present on the national territory of that Member State and all legal relationships within that State.[61]

Accordingly, these provisions typically include domestic regulations of a (semi-) public law nature that intervene in private legal relationships in order to protect the public interest, such as anti-trust regulations, monetary regulations, labour regulations (such as rules on working hours and working conditions),

59 Symeonides 2008b, *op. cit.* pp. 205–206.
60 Art. 16 Rome II Regulation.
61 ECJ Cases C-369/96 and C-376/96, 23 November 1999, [1999] ECR I-8453 (*Arblade*). See also Art. 9 (1) of Regulation (EC) No 593/2008 of the European Parliament and of the Council of 17 June 2008 on the law applicable to contractual obligations (Rome I).

environmental regulations and rules of criminal law.[62] They may also include rules that flow from non-domestic legal sources, like certain provisions of substantive EU law[63] or of public international law, potentially also including certain provisions on the protection of fundamental/human rights.[64]

The extent to which such existing overriding mandatory provisions will be relevant in foreign direct liability cases brought before EU Member State courts remains to be seen. First of all, this exception may according to the text of the Rome II Regulation itself only be applied 'in exceptional circumstances'.[65] At the same time, in line with the contemporary international legal order's state-centred and territorially-based nature, mandatory public law regulation of actors and/or activities outside a state's territory remains an exception.[66] Still, if an EU Member State were to impose, for example, statutory duties for locally based internationally operating business enterprises with respect to the people and planet related impacts of their activities in host countries, such duties could be considered to be overriding mandatory provisions that should find application in foreign direct liability cases brought before the courts in those EU Member States.

Van Hoek states in this respect that

> if the country in which the court sits imposes statutory duties on its corporations with regard to extraterritorial compliance with human rights standards, such duties may override the otherwise applicable law.[67]

She adds to this:

> Some statutes may not stop at prescribing an extraterritorial duty of care, but may stipulate that violation of that duty will lead to civil liability towards the victims, in which case the civil law liability will be based on a mandatory overriding provision as well.[68]

62 See, for instance, Huber 2011, *op. cit.*, pp. 354–356. See also L. Strikwerda, *Inleiding tot het Nederlandse Internationaal Privaatrecht*, Deventer, Kluwer, 2013, pp. 69–70.

63 Compare ECJ Case C-381/98, 9 November 2000, [2000] ECR I-9305 (*Ingmar/Eaton*). See also, more recently but within the scope of contractual obligations (Rome I Regulation): ECJ Case 184–12, 17 October 2013 (*Unamar/Navigation Maritime Bulgare*).

64 See, for instance, with a focus on the European Convention on Human Rights: A. A. H. Van Hoek, 'Transnational Corporate Social Responsibility: Some issues with regard to the Liability of European Corporations for Labour Law Infringements in the Countries of Establishment of their Suppliers', in: Frans Pennings *et al.* (eds.), *Social responsibility in labour relations: European and comparative perspectives*, Alphen aan den Rijn, Kluwer Law International, (2008) p. 147–169. Compare also, within the scope of contractual obligations (Rome I Regulation): Laura M. Van Bochove, 'Overriding Mandatory Rules as a Vehicle for Weaker Party Protection in European Private International Law', 3 *Erasmus Law Review* (2014) 147–156, 150.

65 Recital 32 Rome II Regulation.

66 Compare Augenstein 2010, *op. cit.* p. 72.

67 Van Hoek 2008, *op. cit.* p. 166.

68 *Ibid.*

The hypothetical scenario set out by Van Hoek in 2008 may well become reality at some point in the near to medium-term future. In various European countries legislative initiatives have recently been put forward that seek to transform some of the soft law norms from the UNGPs into mandatory provisions on corporate duties of care in relation to human rights and the environment abroad. In France, there is fierce debate over a legislative proposal on a legal duty of due care (*devoir de vigilance*) for large French business enterprises with regard to people and planet related risks connected with the activities of their subsidiaries, subcontractors and suppliers.[69] In Switzerland, a popular legislative initiative has been put forward requesting an amendment of the Swiss Federal Constitution that would introduce a legally obligatory binding '*responsabilité des entreprises*' for Swiss business enterprises relating to the impact on people and the planet of their own activities and of the activities of business enterprises controlled by them.[70]

The constitutional amendment proposed in the Swiss popular initiative contains a specific provision stating that the provisions dealing with corporate obligations and liabilities 'apply irrespective of the law applicable under private international law'.[71] This provision is meant to ensure that the Swiss legislator would be required to design the constitutional amendment on *responsabilité des entreprises* as an overriding mandatory provision.[72] This is a necessary provision, since on the basis of the applicable Swiss conflict-of-law regime the law applicable to a foreign direct liability claim brought before a Swiss court would in principle be the law of the host country rather than Swiss tort law.[73] Like the Rome II Regulation, however, the Swiss regime provides for the possibility that the court may apply overriding mandatory provisions that are relevant to the subject matter in dispute, irrespective of the law that governs the claim.[74]

Also in Germany, there is debate on the desirability of and possibilities for introducing in German law a statutory duty of care for corporate actors in the human rights context. In a recent study commissioned by a number of German NGOs, a group of German legal experts have set out in detail how such a

69 *Proposition de loi relative au devoir de vigilance des sociétés mères et des entreprises donneuses d'ordre*, no. 708, 23 March 2016, adopted with modifications by the Assemblée Nationale in second reading. Accessible at http://www.assemblee-nationale.fr/14/ta/ta0708.asp.

70 Swiss Coalition for Corporate Justice, *Initiative Multinationales Responsables*, 21 April 2015. Accessible at http://konzern-initiative.ch/initiativtext/?lang=en. It is reported on the website that the initiative has within a year of its launch gathered the number of signatures that is necessary in order for it to be submitted to the Swiss Federal Council and Parliament. They can either accept or reject the amendment or draft a counter-proposal. As long as the initiative is not retracted, it will be put to the popular vote.

71 *Ibid.*, proposed Art. 101a(2)(d).

72 *Ibid.*, explanation of proposed Art. 101a(2)(d).

73 Arts 132, 133(1) and 133(2) *Loi fédérale de droit international privé*. See, in more detail, Enneking *et al.* 2016, pp. 326–327.

74 Art. 18 *Loi fédérale de droit international privé*.

provision could take shape within the German legal system.[75] In this study, ample attention is paid to the fact that such a provision should be shaped as a mandatory overriding provision in order to ensure its applicability in tort cases relating to human rights related harm arising in a host country.[76]

2.3.3.2 Rules of safety and conduct

A further way in which home country legal rules and standards that are relevant to the issue in dispute may find application even in foreign direct liability cases that are decided on the basis of host country rules of tort law, is through the Rome II Regulation's provision on rules of safety and conduct. This provision states that whenever the applicable law is not the law of the country in which the event giving rise to the damage occurred, a court should still take account of 'the rules of safety and conduct which were in force at the place and time of the relevant event'.[77] According to the Explanatory Memorandum, this provision is

> based on the fact that the perpetrator must abide by the rules of safety and conduct in force in the country in which he operates, irrespective of the law applicable to the civil consequences of his action, and that these rules must also be taken into consideration when ascertaining liability.[78]

Examples include local traffic regulations or, more relevant in the context of foreign direct liability cases, rules on safety and hygiene in the workplace.[79]

The provision on rules of safety and conduct may play a role in foreign direct liability cases before EU Member State courts dealing with the liability of EU-based parent companies for harm caused to human and environmental interests in non-EU host countries, as it allows the court to take into account home country behavioural standards that may be stricter than those in the host country, even when the law of the host country is applicable to the case.[80] Taking account of the rules of safety and conduct of the home country is not the same as applying them, however. They should be taken into account by the court as a matter of fact and insofar as is appropriate, 'for example when assessing the seriousness of the fault or the author's good or bad faith for the purposes of the measure of damages'.[81]

75 Remo Klinger *et al.*, *Verankerung menschenrechtlicher Sorgfaltspflichten von Unternehmen im deutschen Recht*, March 2016. Accessible at https://germanwatch.org/de/download/14745.pdf.
76 *Ibid.*, pp. 71–76.
77 Art. 17 Rome II Regulation.
78 Explanatory Memorandum p. 25.
79 Compare Van Hoek 2008, *op. cit.* p. 166.
80 Compare Symeonides 2008b, *op. cit.* pp. 211–215.
81 *Ibid.*

Accordingly, home country rules on safety and hygiene in the workplace are not applied as such, but for instance used to determine an employer's duty of care vis-à-vis his employees.[82] Similarly, it seems that the provision on rules of safety and conduct does not create an opportunity to replace the applicable rules on tort law of the *lex loci damni* with any (stricter) liability rules applicable at the place where the events giving rise to the damage occurred that would pertain specifically to the conduct in dispute. Van Hoek notes in this respect that

> it seems clear that Article 17 should not be construed in such a way as to contain a special rules on the tortiousness of the behaviour based on the *lex locus actus* [i.e. home country tort law]. Such *depeçage* would run counter to Article 15 of the Regulation which provides that all major elements of tortious liability (the tortiousness of the act as such, liability and exceptions thereto, the assessment of damages etc.) are covered by the law applicable on the basis of Article 4 ff.[83]

The provision on rules of safety and conduct may also cover unwritten rules pertaining to proper social conduct, guidelines and soft law norms.[84] This is important, as it opens up the possibility that EU Member State courts dealing with foreign direct liability claims against EU Member State-based companies take account of behavioural standards of safety and conduct that flow from instruments like the UNGPs and the OECD Guidelines for Multinational Enterprises.[85] In addition, the provision may potentially also be used by EU Member State courts dealing with foreign direct liability cases to take into account any domestic rules of criminal law that pertain to the extraterritorial violations of human or environmental interests that are at issue in the cases brought before them.[86] Examples of such provisions are those criminalizing the direct or indirect participation by companies in modern slavery at home and abroad as exist in Dutch law,[87] or those criminalizing the participation by private military and security companies (PMSCs) in human rights abuses committed in armed conflicts abroad as exist in Swiss law.[88]

82 *Ibid.*
83 *Ibid.*
84 See, in more detail, Enneking 2012, *op. cit.* pp. 220–222.
85 *Ibid.*
86 Van Hoek 2008, *op. cit.* p. 166.
87 See, in more detail, A.-J. L.M. Schaap, *Chocolade met een Bittere Nasmaak – De Strafrechtelijke Aansprakelijkheid van Nederlandse Ondernemingen voor Moderne Slavernij*, blog, Utrecht Centre for Accountability and Liability Law, 21 June 2016. Accessible at http://blog.ucall.nl/index.php/2016/06/chocolade-met-een-bittere-nasmaak-de-strafrechtelijke-aansprakelijkheid-van-nederlandse-ondernemingen-voor-moderne-slavernij/; Enneking *et al.* 2016, *op. cit.* pp. 146–147.
88 See, in more detail, Enneking *et al.* 2016, *op. cit.* pp. 336–337.

Van Hoek notes in this respect, however, that

> in those cases, reliance on Article 16 [on overriding mandatory provisions] might be preferred as that provision allows for outright application of the forum's mandatory provisions. Moreover, Article 16 allows such application in all circumstances in which the rules of the forum claim application whereas Article 17 only refers to rules of the *locus actus* and hence is incapable of covering all cases in which there is criminal jurisdiction within the forum.[89]

2.3.3.3 Public policy

Finally, under the Rome II regime EU Member State courts may by way of exception refuse to apply a provision of host country tort law in foreign direct liability cases brought before them, where (the application of) the provision in question is manifestly incompatible with fundamental principles and values of the legal order (*ordre public*) of the forum.[90] This may provide an important minimum guarantee (or 'emergency brake')[91] in foreign direct liability cases that are brought before EU Member State courts but governed by host country law, especially since fundamental human rights principles, whether ensuing from international or domestic law, are considered to be part of the public policy of the forum.[92] As such, it is conceivable that, under this provision, EU Member State courts will for example refuse to apply provisions of host country law that would condone child labour or amount to serious violations of (international) human rights norms.[93]

The actual extent of this role for the public policy exception in foreign direct liability cases brought before EU Member State courts is not unlimited, however. First of all, the use of the public policy exception is meant to remain exceptional; its application in a particular case may be subject to review by the ECJ. The fact that, in the eyes of the court seized of the matter, the applicable rules of the host country are wrong as to their substance and conclusion, is not a sufficient reason for invoking public policy, not even if the incorrectness is manifest.[94] There has to be a conflict with fundamental legal principles for the court seized of the matter to be allowed to refuse to apply a host country regulation on the basis of the public policy exception, and apply its own law instead.[95] The ECJ, for example, found such conflict in a case in which a defendant's

89 Van Hoek 2008, *op. cit.* pp. 166–167.
90 Art. 26 Rome II Regulation.
91 Castermans & Van der Weide 2010, *op. cit.* p. 54.
92 See, in more detail for instance, Augenstein 2010, *op. cit.* pp. 72–73; Van Hoek 2008, *op. cit.* pp. 167–168.
93 Augenstein 2010, *op. cit.* p. 73; Van Hoek 2008, *op. cit.* pp. 167–168.
94 ECJ Case C-38/98, 11 May 2000, [2000] ECR I-02973 (*Renault/Maxicar*).
95 Compare recital 32 Rome II Regulation and Explanatory Memorandum, *op. cit.* p. 28. See also, in more detail, Enneking 2008, *op. cit.* pp. 306–307.

right to defend himself before his court of origin, as recognized by the European Convention on Human Rights, had been manifestly breached.[96]

It should be noted, however, that where it comes to the norms ensuing from international human rights conventions, account needs to be taken of the fact that international conventions in principle apply only within the territories of their Member States. Whether they could be applied ‘extraterritorially’ to actors and/or activities in non-Member States is disputable. The question may be raised, therefore, as to what role for instance the substantive human rights norms laid down in the European Convention on Human Rights (ECHR) (as opposed to procedural norms like Article 6 ECHR) could play in relation to the determination of the applicable law in foreign direct liability cases brought before EU Member State courts that pertain to human rights violations perpetrated in non-European host countries. Van Hoek asserts in this respect that

> when the application of foreign law leads to a result which is unacceptable if measured against the standards (rather than the rules) of the ECHR, the public policy exception intervenes and *lex fori* is applied instead. If the applicable foreign law does not provide a remedy for gross violations of human rights taking place within the territory, this would be a violation of such a Convention standard.[97]

Still, in the particular context of foreign direct liability cases, where application of host country law may lead to fundamentally different outcomes with respect to standards of care in relation to the protection of human and environmental interests, including fundamental human rights standards, the public policy exception may well prove instrumental.[98]

2.3.4 Discussion

In foreign direct liability cases brought before EU Member State courts, the issue of applicable law is largely determined by EU law in the form of the Rome II Regulation. The EU Member States’ national rules on conflict-of-law in tort cases will in principle only play a role in those foreign direct liability cases that fall outside the temporal scope of the Rome II Regulation due to the fact that they pertain to events giving rise to damage that occurred before 11 January 2009. As time progresses, however, more and more of these cases will fall within the temporal scope of the Rome II Regulation.

Under the rules set out in the Rome II Regulation, foreign direct liability claims brought before EU Member State courts will in most cases be decided not on the basis of home country tort law but on the basis of the rules on

96 ECJ Case C-7/98, 28 March 2000, [2000] ECR I-01935 (*Krombach/Bamberski*).
97 Van Hoek 2008, *op. cit.* p. 167.
98 See also Augenstein 2010, *op. cit.* p. 76.

non-contractual liability that apply in the host country. This is likely to be different only where the case pertains to environmental damage (or to damage sustained by persons or property as a result of such damage) and where the event giving rise to the damage can be said to have taken place in the home country of the corporate defendant (where relevant decisions have been taken, group policies have been imposed, supervision of host country activities should have taken place, human rights due diligence should have been exercised, etc). In that case, the victim is presented with the option of choosing the applicability of the law of the home country instead of that of the host country.

The possibility of pursuing foreign direct liability cases in the EU Member States on the basis of home country tort law is of fundamental importance. It determines whether EU Member States can deploy their national systems of tort law as a much needed regulatory instrument that can promote international corporate social responsibility and, more in particular, corporate respect for human rights by EU-based internationally operating business enterprises operating in developing host countries. At the same time, it also determines the possibilities for host country based individuals and communities who have suffered harm as a result of the activities of EU-based internationally operating business enterprises to ensure, through this type of litigation, that the level of protection of their environmental and human rights interests is adequate and not fundamentally different from that afforded to those living in the EU home countries of the business enterprises involved.[99]

The law that is applicable to a foreign direct liability case covers issues such as the standard of liability, the available remedies, the calculation of damages as well as rules determining the burden of proof. This means that the development in EU Member States of statutory provisions or case law with respect to duties of care for internationally operating business enterprises in relation to human and environmental interests in non-EU host countries will only have meaning and effect if those provisions and precedents may find application in foreign direct liability cases brought before EU Member State courts. It also means that the remedies or levels of damages or alleviations of the burden of proof that may be afforded to EU citizens and communities in litigation over violations of environmental and human rights norms will only be available to victims from non-EU host states in foreign direct liability cases if home country tort law is applied in foreign direct liability cases brought before EU Member State courts.[100]

In the end, this is thus a matter of justice and fairness, as is also expressed by one of the British legal counsel of a large group of Ivorians who sought to hold the Anglo-Dutch Petroleum trader Trafigura liable before an English

99 See, in more detail, Enneking 2012, pp. 134–135, 137–140, 152–155, 301–307, 504–521; Enneking 2008.

100 *Ibid.*

court for the harm caused by the Probo Koala toxic waste dumping incident in 2006:

> Although the events took place thousands of miles away, it is right that this British company is made to account for its actions by the British courts, and made to pay British levels of damages for what happened. A British company should act in Abidjan in exactly the same way as they would act in Abergavenny.[101]

However, it is also – and increasingly so – a matter of policy, as is underlined by the growing willingness among European policymakers to consider the introduction of legal norms to promote international corporate social responsibility and corporate respect for human rights in host countries by 'their' internationally operating business enterprises.[102] This is exemplified by the ongoing debates on the introduction of statutory human rights due diligence obligations for internationally operating business enterprises – combined with the possibility of civil liability for violations thereof – in France, Switzerland and – more recently – Germany.[103] These developments have in turn prompted the launch of a green card initiative by members from eight EU Member State Parliaments calling for the EU-wide introduction of a duty of care towards individuals and communities whose human rights and local environment are affected by the activities of EU-based companies.[104]

At the same time, EU Member State courts are demonstrating an increasing willingness to consider the possibility that the parent company of a corporate group may owe a duty of care towards third parties (workers, neighbours, communities) whose environmental, human rights and/or health and safety related interests are negatively affected by the operations of its subsidiaries, and that it may be liable in case of a breach of that duty. This is evidenced by the case of *Chandler v Cape*, a 2012 English case in which a parent company of a corporate group was held liable, both at first instance and on appeal, for asbestos-related injuries suffered by

101 See, with further references, Enneking 2008, pp. 284–285.

102 See, in more detail, Enneking *et al.* 2016, pp. 157–343.

103 *Proposition de loi relative au devoir de vigilance des sociétés mères et des entreprises donneuses d'ordre*, no. 708, 23 March 2016, adopted with modifications by the Assemblée Nationale in second reading, accessible at http://www.assemblee-nationale.fr/14/ta/ta0708.asp; Swiss Coalition for Corporate Justice, *Initiative Multinationales Responsables*, 21 April 2015 accessible at http://konzern-initiative.ch/initiativtext/?lang=en; Klinger *et al.* 2016, *op. cit.* See, in more detail, Enneking *et al.* 2016, pp. 236–237, 330–332.

104 See, for instance, ECCJ, *Members of 8 European Parliaments support duty of care legislation for EU corporations*, 31 May 2016, accessible at http://corporatejustice.org/news/132-members-of-8-european-parliaments-support-duty-of-care-legislation-for-eu-corporations; Sherpa, *Parlimentarians from all the EU commit to strengthen the social responsibility of multinational companies*, 18 May 2016, accessible at https://www.asso-sherpa.org/parliamentarians-from-all-the-eu-commit-to-strengthen-the-social-responsibility-of-multinational-companies.

an employee of one of its subsidiaries as it was considered to have breached a duty of care owed to the employee.[105] It is also evidenced by the judgments of the Hague District Court and the Hague Court of Appeal in the Dutch Shell Nigeria case, as both courts held, in response to the corporate defendants' assertion that the claims against the parent company were 'evidently without merit', that parent company liability was a possible scenario also in the case at hand.[106]

These developments in (prospective) legislation and case law in a number of the EU Member States underline the importance of having the possibility of applying home country tort law in foreign direct liability cases brought before EU Member State courts. The Rome II Regulation's special rule on environmental damage may provide a basis for this. However, this basis is not only uncertain, due to the fact that it remains unclear for now whether it may be relied on in foreign direct liability cases, but also very narrow, as it would only be available in cases involving environmental damage or damage sustained by persons or property as a result thereof.

As a consequence, the application and enforcement through foreign direct liability cases of any legal norms developed in the EU Member States to promote international corporate social responsibility and corporate respect for human rights in host countries, remains dependent on the applicability of one of the Rome II Regulation's other exceptions. The exceptions as regards overriding mandatory provisions of the law of the forum country and as regards the public policy of the forum country could potentially be relevant in this regard. According to the Regulation, however, these are only to be applied in exceptional circumstances,[107] which means that they can only play a limited role in this context. The same is true for the provision on rules of safety and conduct that are in force at the place of the event giving rise to liability, as these rules need only be taken into account by the court as a matter of fact and insofar as the court deems appropriate.

With respect to the two exceptions mentioned, it should be noted that the Committee of Ministers of the Council of Europe in its 2016 Recommendation on human rights and business has recommended:

> Member States should apply such legislative or other appropriate measures as may be necessary to ensure that their domestic courts refrain from

105 *Chandler v Cape plc* [2012] EWCA Civ 525. See, in more detail for instance, Siel Demeyere, 'Liability of a Mother Company for its Subsidiary in French, Belgian, and English Law', 3 *European Review of Private Law* (2015) 385–413; Enneking *et al.* 2016, *op. cit.* pp. 292–296.

106 See, for instance: The Hague District Court, 30 December 2009, ELI:NL:RBSGR:2009:BK8616 (oil spill near Oruma), paras. 3.2-3.3; The Hague District Court, 30 January 2013, ECLI:NL:RBDHA:2013:BY9850 (oil spill near Oruma), para. 4.4; The Hague Court of Appeal, 18 December 2015, ECLI:NL:GHDHA:2015:3588 (oil spill near Oruma), paras, 2.1-2.8.

107 Recital 32 Rome II Regulation.

applying a law that is incompatible with their international obligations, in particular those stemming from the applicable international human rights standards.[108]

A more structural solution may lie in an extension of the scope of the Rome II Regulation's special rule on environmental damage to human rights related damage as well as, possibly, health and safety related damage. After all, many of the policy rationales prompting the introduction of the special rule on environmental damage can be said to also exist – or even more so – with respect to these types of damage if they are caused by the operations of EU-based business enterprises. Also in these cases, the exclusive connection to the place where the damage is sustained would mean that a victim from a low-protection host country would not enjoy the higher level of protection that may be available in the EU Member State home countries of the business enterprises involved.[109]

Extending the scope of the special rule on environmental damage in this way would be crucial to enabling EU (Member States') policies aimed at contributing to raising the general level of protection not only with respect to environmental matters but also with respect to human rights and health and safety related matters. In light of the fact that also in cases resulting in human rights related damage or health and safety related damage, the author of the damage (unlike other torts or delicts) generally derives an economic benefit from his harmful activity, the focus of the special rule on environmental damage alone may even seem arbitrary.[110] A broader possibility of discriminating in favour of the person sustaining the damage in this broader category of cases would thus strongly contribute to the realization of EU (Member States') policies on international corporate social responsibility and business respect for human rights.

2.4 Procedural rules and practical circumstances[111]

A factor that tends to have a crucial impact on the feasibility of foreign direct liability claims is formed by the relevant procedural rules and practical circumstances under which these claims can be brought before Western society home country courts.

One of the features that is characteristic of foreign direct liability cases is that the parties to these cases are typically unevenly matched, as the corporate defendants are usually in a much better position than the host country plaintiffs with respect to both information and finances. The fact that there is typically

108 Council of Europe Committee of Ministers, Recommendation CM/Rec(2016)3 of the Committee of Ministers to Member States on human rights and business, no. 40.

109 Compare Explanatory Memorandum, *op. cit.* pp. 19–20.

110 *Ibid.*

111 This section is largely derived from: Enneking *et al.* 2016, *op. cit.*; Enneking 2012, *op. cit.*

little transparency with respect to the often complex group and operational structures of the multinational corporations involved, and also on the way in which their international operations are actually coordinated, controlled, managed and/or supervised, may significantly hamper host country plaintiffs seeking to hold them accountable. At the same time, the fact that the host country plaintiffs usually only have very limited financial means at their disposal from which to finance these often complex, expensive and drawn-out legal procedures, tends to put them at a significant disadvantage vis-à-vis their corporate opponents.[112]

Consequently, there are a number of issues that tend to be of particular relevance in this context. These include: 1) the financial aspects of bringing foreign direct liability claims, also considering their typical complex and drawn-out nature; and the availability of expert legal and practical assistance; 2) the possibilities for bringing collective actions; 3) circumstances relating to the collection of evidence and burden of proof.[113] As matters of evidence (with the exception of rules which raise presumptions of law or determine the burden of proof)[114] and procedure fall outside the material scope of the Rome II Regulation,[115] these issues are largely determined by the procedural rules and practical circumstances of the EU Member State where the foreign direct liability case is brought.

2.4.1 General observations

The fact that, up until now, foreign direct liability cases have nowhere been as prevalent as in the US, is sometimes explained as resulting from the fact that the litigation cultures in other Western societies are, by comparison, less conducive to this type of litigation.[116] The US legal culture of adversarial legalism and its tradition of public interest and impact litigation, accompanied by plaintiff-friendly rules of civil procedure and litigation practices, are unique to the US and unlikely to be found elsewhere.[117] In fact, the US litigation culture is often depicted outside the US as being excessive and something to be avoided rather than welcomed. Disadvantages that are commonly perceived to be associated with it include: over-precaution, which may lead to high costs for potential

112 See, in more detail, Enneking 2012, *op. cit.* pp. 114–116.

113 Enneking *et al.* 2016, *op. cit.* pp. 111–126; Enneking 2012, *op. cit.* pp. 136–137 *et seq.*

114 Art. 22(1) Rome II Regulation.

115 Art. 3 Rome II Regulation.

116 See, for instance, Beth Stephens, 'Translating *Filártiga*: a Comparative and International Law Analysis of Domestic Remedies for International Human Rights Violations', 1 *Yale Journal of International Law* (2002) 2–57, 17–34.

117 Enneking 2012, *op. cit.* pp. 191–194; Ulrich Magnus, 'Why is US tort law so different?', 1 *Journal of European Tort Law* (2010) 102–124, 119–120; Stephens 2002 *op. cit.* pp. 24–27; Robert A. Kagan, *Adversarial Legalism: The American Way of Law*, Cambridge MA, Harvard University Press, 2001.

tortfeasors, deterrence of economically valuable activities and restraints on innovation; abuse of civil procedures for unmeritorious claims, which may lead to high societal costs and so-called 'blackmail settlements'; insurance issues; and high transaction costs.

Generally speaking, a public interest related litigation infrastructure similar to the US model has failed to materialize in Europe, where public issues have tended to be addressed through societal dialogue and government intervention rather than through civil litigation. As a consequence, law firms specializing in public interest cases have remained exceptions and of the numerous European NGOs involved in issues of international corporate social responsibility, only a few are seeking to address issues of corporate wrongdoing in this respect through litigation rather than through dialogue with businesses and governments. Overall, the combination of procedural and practical features of civil litigation systems in the EU Member States tends to be less favourable to plaintiffs in foreign direct liability cases than is the case in the US.[118]

2.4.2 *The financing of claims, collective redress and access to evidence*

Notwithstanding the fact that the European civil law systems are often said to be converging, differences in legal culture between the different countries remain quite pervasive.[119] This also means that the extent to which procedural rules and practical circumstances in the EU Member States are as conducive to the pursuit of foreign direct liability claims as the US civil litigation system, varies from country to country. However, the general picture is that none of the EU Member States features a combination of procedural rules and practical circumstances that is as conducive to the pursuit of foreign direct liability cases as the US civil litigation system.[120]

Compared to the other European systems, the UK legal system at this point seems most conducive for this type of litigation, which (at least partly) explains why up until now the far majority of (tort law based) European foreign direct liability claims have been pursued there.[121] Features that render English courts a desirable forum for plaintiffs seeking to pursue foreign direct liability claims include the possibility for plaintiffs to enter into contingency fee arrangements with their legal representatives, the availability of collective redress

118 See, in more detail, Enneking 2012, *op. cit.* pp. 194–197.

119 See, for instance, C. C. Van Dam, 'Who is Afraid of Diversity? – Cultural Diversity, European Co-operation and European Tort Law', 2 *King's Law Journal* (2009) 281–308.

120 J. Zerk, *Corporate Liability for Gross Human Rights Abuses*, Report prepared for the Office of the UN High Commissioner on Human Rights, 2014. Accessible at http://www.ohchr.org/Documents/Issues/Business/DomesticLawRemedies/StudyDomesticeLawRemedies.pdf, pp. 79–87; Enneking 2012, pp. 194–202.

121 Compare Enneking *et al.* 2016, *op. cit.* pp. 439–442.

mechanisms such as the group litigation order and the representative action, and relatively liberal rules on disclosure and discovery of evidence.[122]

In most European civil law systems, the losing party to a lawsuit must bear the costs of the winning party, a circumstance that may restrain prospective plaintiffs from initiating novel or otherwise risky civil cases. Furthermore, contingency fee arrangements are not permitted in most European civil law countries; instead, lawyers tend to charge fixed fees. This does bring with it the advantage, however, that lawyers are unlikely to refuse potential cases on the basis that they are unlikely to result in large damages awards. Also, as a counterbalance to the rule on litigation costs and the unavailability of contingency fees, many European civil law systems provide legal aid to poor plaintiffs who need financial assistance in order to be able to bring their claims, at least where those claims have a reasonable prospect of success. In some countries, however, legal aid is only available to residents or nationals of the forum state, which excludes plaintiffs in foreign direct liability cases.[123]

Furthermore, corollaries to the US-type class action, in which a single procedure may represent a group of claims and/or defendants (if those can be said to form a class and to be affected in almost the same way) in such a way as to allow for a reduction of costs and risks and/or to provide incentives to pursue even those tort cases that involve such small amounts of damages that they would not be pursued separately, are unavailable in most European legal systems. However, the possibilities for collective redress in Europe have expanded significantly in recent years. Most European legal systems now provide for some form of collective action, in the sense that representative organizations may pursue civil litigation on behalf of a group of persons or certain interests and/or in the sense that multiple claims or defendants may be bundled into one procedure.[124] Still, in many countries the availability of collective actions is restricted to particular subject matter areas that are often not relevant in foreign direct liability cases (like consumer law or competition law), or entail restrictions as to standing and available remedies.[125]

Finally, discovery rules in most European legal systems generally do not offer plaintiffs the same broad possibilities for requesting information from the defendants as do the rules on pre-trial discovery in the US. A general procedural duty to present all documents that are requested by the other party on the basis

122 See, in more detail, Enneking *et al.* 2016, *op. cit.* pp. 299–301; Zerk 2014, pp. 194–202.

123 See, in more detail, Enneking *et al.* 2016, *op. cit.* pp. 111–126, 179–182, 213–215, 256–258, 299–301, 333–335; Zerk 2014, pp. 194–202; Magnus 2010, *op. cit.* pp. 112–115.

124 See in more detail, for example, Christopher Hodges, *The reform of class and representative actions in European legal systems* (2008) Hart: Oxford

125 See, in more detail: Enneking *et al.* 2016, *op. cit.* pp. 111–126, 179–182, 213–215, 256–258, 299–301, 333–335; Zerk 2014, pp. 194–202; Magnus 2010, *op. cit.* pp. 115–116.

of their potential relevance to the case does not exist in most European civil law systems. Instead, parties may under certain conditions have a right to request disclosure of documents and/or courts may order such disclosure where considered necessary. However, these possibilities for document disclosure tend to be quite restrictive, meaning that the possibilities for plaintiffs in foreign direct liability cases brought before EU Member State courts to get access to relevant documents that are not in their own hands remain (very) limited, at least in the civil law systems.[126]

2.4.3 The role of Article 6 ECHR

It is important to point out the role that the right to a fair trial, which is protected by Article 6 of the ECHR, may potentially play a role in foreign direct liability cases brought before EU Member State courts. This provision applies to any civil (or criminal) procedure initiated before an EU Member State court, regardless of whether it is a purely domestic procedure or whether the procedure has international aspects. It entails an obligation on the Member States to ensure that civil trials within their territories are accessible, fair and speedy, which obliges them for instance to ensure that (civil) litigants have a right of access to their courts that is both effective and practical. The European Court of Human Rights (ECtHR) has stated in this respect:

> Article 6 §1 secures to everyone the right to have any claim relating to his civil rights and obligations brought before a court or tribunal. In this way the Article embodies the 'right to a court', of which the right of access, that is the right to institute proceedings before courts in civil matters, constitutes one aspect only. To this are added the guarantees laid down by Article 6 §1 as regards both the organisation and composition of the court, and the conduct of the proceedings. In sum, the whole makes up the right to a fair hearing.[127]

Article 6 may act as a minimum threshold when it comes to the length (duration) of civil proceedings and when it comes to the costs involved. It has for instance been interpreted by the ECtHR to encompass an obligation, under certain circumstances, to enable plaintiffs in civil cases to acquire legal aid.[128]

126 See, in more detail, Enneking *et al.* 2016, *op. cit.* pp. 111–126, 179–182, 213–215, 256–258, 299–301, 333–335; Zerk 2014, pp. 194–202; Magnus 2010, *op. cit.* p. 116–117. See also, with a focus on impediments to transparency in Dutch foreign direct liability cases: Enneking 2013, *op. cit.*

127 European Court of Human Rights, 21 February 1975, 18 Eur.Ct.H.R. (Ser. A) 1975 (*Golder/United Kingdom*).

128 See, for instance, European Court of Human Rights, 9 October 1979, 32 EurCtHR (Ser. A) 1979 (*Airey/Ireland*), where the Court held, inter alia, that '[a]rticle 6 § 1 may sometimes compel the State to provide for the assistance of a lawyer when such assistance

Furthermore, it also imposes duties on the ECHR Member States to make sure for instance that their domestic rules on evidence do not in practice violate the equality of arms principle that ensues from Article 6. According to the ECtHR:

> each party must be afforded a reasonable opportunity to present his case – including his evidence – under conditions that do not place him at a substantial disadvantage vis-à-vis his opponent.[129]

It should be noted, however, that the Member States are left with a margin of appreciation as to how to achieve these results, which means that not all limitations to access to court or equality of arms are automatically incompatible with the Convention.

It seems that Article 6 ECHR may potentially provide an important minimum guarantee to host country plaintiffs in foreign direct liability cases who find that certain features of the systems of civil procedure in the European home countries where they bring their claims seriously hamper their right to a fair trial. This may be the case for instance where excessively high litigation costs, the unavailability of affordable legal assistance or legal aid, or the evidentiary rules of the forum make it practically impossible for them to pursue their claims. These factors gain significance in light of the inequality of arms that typically exists between the host country plaintiffs in these cases and their corporate opponents as regards financial scope, level of organization, and access to relevant information.[130]

Illustrative of the role that Article 6 ECHR may play in this respect is a UK defamation case between a multinational corporation and NGO campaigners. In this case, the ECtHR held that the state had a responsibility to ensure equality of arms between the parties to the dispute and that, in light of the disparity between the respective levels of legal assistance enjoyed by the parties to this particular case, the state's refusal to grant legal aid to the NGO campaigners imposed an unfair restriction on their ability to present an effective defence.[131]

In the Dutch Shell Nigeria case, Article 6 ECHR was raised by the plaintiffs in relation to their limited possibilities for obtaining evidence that was in the hands of their corporate opponents under the relatively strict Dutch civil procedural regime on the production of exhibits. The court refused to accept their argument, however, holding that the restrictions of the Dutch regime are in

proves indispensable for an effective access to court either because legal representation is rendered compulsory, as is done by the domestic law of certain Contracting States for various types of litigation, or by reason of the complexity of the procedure or of the case' (p. 15).

129 European Court of Human Rights, 27 October 1993, [1993] ECHR 49 14448/88 (*Dombo Beheer/The Netherlands*), para. 33.

130 See, in more detail, Enneking 2012, pp. 114–116.

131 European Court of Human Rights, 15 February 2005, [2005] ECHR 103 (*Steel and Morris/United Kingdom*), paras 59–71.

principle compatible with Article 6 ECHR and the equality of arms principle, except where special circumstances dictate otherwise. According to the court, the plaintiffs failed to prove the existence of such special circumstances under which a deviation from the regular application of the Dutch regime on the production of exhibits was warranted.[132]

2.4.4 Discussion

Since they fall outside the material scope of the Rome II Regulation, the issue of procedural rules and practical circumstances is mainly determined not by EU law but by the national procedural rules and litigation practices that are in place in the EU Member State countries where foreign direct liability cases are brought before a court. The issue is of crucial importance, however, as it determines whether victims will in practice have any chance of successfully pursuing a foreign direct liability case before an EU Member State court.[133]

According to the UNGPs, states are under an obligation to

> take appropriate steps to ensure the effectiveness of domestic judicial mechanisms when addressing business-related human rights abuses, including considering ways to reduce legal, practical and other relevant barriers that could lead to a denial of access to remedy.[134]

The UNGPs stress that many of such barriers 'are the result of, or compounded by, the frequent imbalances between the parties to business-related human rights claims, such as in their financial resources, access to information and expertise'.[135]

An example of a legal barrier, according to the UNGPs, is the situation that 'claimants face a denial of justice in a host State and cannot access home State courts regardless of the merits of the claim'.[136] As regards practical and procedural barriers that may prevent victims of corporate human rights abuse from getting access to judicial remedies, the UNGPs give four specific examples:

> 1. The costs of bringing claims go beyond being an appropriate deterrent to unmeritorious cases and/or cannot be reduced to reasonable levels through Government support, "market-based" mechanisms (such as litigation insurance and legal fee structures), or other means;

132 See, for instance, The Hague District Court, 14 September 2011, ECLI:NL:RBSGR:2011:BU3535 (oil spill near Oruma), para. 4.16. See also, in more detail, L. F. H. Enneking, 'Multinationals and Transparency in Foreign Direct Liability Cases', 3 *The Dovenschmidt Quarterly* (2013) 134–147.

133 See, in more detail, Enneking 2012, pp. 136–137, 187–191, 307–309.

134 Principle 26 UN Guiding Principles, *op. cit.*

135 Commentary Principle 26 UN Guiding Principles, *op. cit.*

136 *Ibid.*

2. claimants experience difficulty in securing legal representation, due to a lack of resources or of other incentives for lawyers to advise claimants in this area;
3. there are inadequate options for aggregating claims or enabling representative proceedings (such as class actions and other collective action procedures), and this prevents effective remedy for individual claimants;
4. State prosecutors lack adequate resources, expertise and support to meet the State's own obligations to investigate individual and business involvement in human rights-related crimes.[137]

Considering the focus of this book on procedural rules and practical circumstances that are likely to pose the main barriers for access of victims of corporate human rights (and environmental) abuse to civil law remedies before EU Member State courts, the criminal law related fourth example will be left aside here. The other three examples of practical and procedural barriers that may prevent victims of corporate human rights (and environmental) abuse from getting access to judicial remedies, however, all appear to be present to some extent in many of the EU Member States. Especially in foreign direct liability cases, where there is typically a significant inequality of arms as regards financial scope, level of organization and access to relevant information between the plaintiffs (victims from non-EU and mostly developing host countries) and their corporate opponents (large EU-based internationally operating enterprises), this significantly affects the feasibility of successfully pursuing these cases before EU Member State courts.

In many of the EU Member States, significant thresholds exist with respect to the costs associated with the pursuit of these often complex cases, often in combination with limited (or no) possibilities of entering into contingency fee agreements (or similar outcome-related fee arrangements) with legal representatives, and limited (or, for non-nationals, no) availability of legal aid. In addition, the options for pursuing collective actions (i.e. group actions or representative actions) in this particular context tend to be limited (except perhaps for claims dealing with environmental harm), whereas restrictive rules on document disclosure tend to make it very difficult (if not impossible) for the plaintiffs in these cases to furnish the court with the evidence needed to substantiate their claims.

It should be noted that the Committee of Ministers of the Council of Europe in its 2016 Recommendation on human rights and business has recommended with respect to these particular procedural and practical thresholds, that:

> Member States should consider adopting measures that allow entities such as foundations, associations, trade unions and other organisations to bring claims on behalf of alleged victims; Member States should consider possible

137 *Ibid.*

> solutions for the collective determination of similar cases in respect of business-related human rights abuses; Member States should consider revising their civil procedures where the applicable rules impede access to information in the possession of the defendant or a third party if such information is relevant to substantiating victims' claims of business-related human rights abuses, with due regard for confidentiality considerations.[138]

All in all, none of the EU Member states features a combination of legal culture, procedural rules and practical circumstances that is as conducive to the pursuit of foreign direct liability cases as the US civil litigation system. The UK legal system at this point seems most conducive for this type of litigation, which (at least partly) explains why the far majority of (tort law based) European foreign direct liability claims have so far been pursued before English courts. In procedures before any of the EU Member State courts, the right to a fair trial as laid down in Article 6 ECHR may potentially provide an important minimum guarantee where excessively high litigation costs, the unavailability of affordable legal assistance or legal aid, or the evidentiary rules of the forum make it practically impossible to pursue foreign direct liability cases.

However, not all limitations on the access to court are automatically incompatible with the Convention, which means that courts will probably only under (very) special circumstances consider restrictive procedural rules or practical circumstances to be in violation of Article 6 ECHR. It should be noted, however, that the Committee of Ministers of the Council of Europe in its 2016 Recommendation on human rights and business has recommended in this respect:

> When alleged victims of business-related human rights abuses bring civil claims related to such abuses against business enterprises, Member States should ensure that their legal systems sufficiently guarantee an equality of arms within the meaning of Article 6 of the European Convention on Human Rights. In particular, they should provide in their legal systems for legal aid schemes regarding claims concerning such abuses. Such legal aid should be obtainable in a manner that is practical and effective.[139]

Still, the existence in most EU Member States of procedural rules and practical circumstances that render the pursuit of foreign direct liability cases very difficult or, in some cases, even impossible is a matter of serious concern when it comes to ensuring access to justice in EU Member State courts for victims of corporate human rights and environmental abuse by EU-based internationally operating

138 Council of Europe Committee of Ministers, Recommendation CM/Rec(2016)3 of the Committee of Ministers to Member States on human rights and business, nos. 39, 42, 43.

139 Council of Europe Committee of Ministers, Recommendation CM/Rec(2016)3 of the Committee of Ministers to Member States on human rights and business, no. 41.

business enterprises. It is an issue that needs to be addressed not just at the level of the individual Member States but also at the EU level, if the EU is serious about realizing EU policies or supporting EU Member States' policies on international corporate social responsibility and business respect for human rights. And even though EU competences in the field of civil procedural law are inherently limited, EU involvement in this field is not unprecedented, as there have been various attempts over the past years to strengthen the enforcement role of the Member States' systems of civil law in fields such as competition law and consumer law.[140]

A relevant outcome is the Commission's 2013 initiative on collective redress, which seeks to promote national redress mechanisms for the enforcement of EU law in, among other areas, the field of environmental protection.[141] This raises the question of to what extent the EU considers the promotion of international corporate social responsibility and business respect for human rights by EU-based internationally operating business enterprises in non-EU host countries an EU matter and a priority at this point in time. If so, the reduction of practical and procedural barriers in the EU Member States that may lead to a denial of access to justice before EU Member State courts for victims of corporate human rights and environmental abuse, regardless of the merits of the claims, should be one of its main priorities in the years to come.

2.5 Conclusions and recommendations

One of the main focal points of the debates in the EU Member States on access to judicial remedies for victims of corporate human rights abuses is the contemporary trend towards foreign direct liability cases: transnational (civil) liability claims against internationally operating business enterprises in relation to harm caused to people and the planet in the course of their operations – or those of their subsidiaries or supply chain partners – in developing host countries. Over the past two decades, the prevalence of this type of litigation before EU Member State courts has strongly increased, from a mere handful of cases in the 1990s to a total of around 40 cases pursued in various EU Member States up until now – and counting.

Whether these foreign direct liability cases can play a role in providing victims of corporate human rights and environmental abuse with access to judicial remedies before EU Member State courts is dependent on a number of factors that determine the feasibility of these cases. These include, among others, the question of what law EU Member State courts should apply in determining the validity of these claims, and the question of whether there are barriers inherent in

140 See, in more detail, Enneking 2012, *op. cit.* pp. 307–309.

141 Commission recommendation of 11 June 2013 on common principles for injunctive and compensatory collective redress mechanisms in the Member States concerning violations of rights granted under Union Law, 2013/396/EU, *OJEU* L 201/60 (26 July 2013).

the procedural rules and practical circumstances in the EU member States that may prevent these cases from being pursued, regardless of their merits. In foreign direct liability cases brought before EU Member State courts, the issue of applicable law is largely determined by EU law in the form of the Rome II Regulation. Under this Regulation, foreign direct liability claims brought before EU Member State courts will in most cases be decided not on the basis of home country tort law but on the basis of host country tort law. This is likely to be different only where the case pertains to environmental damage (or to damage sustained by persons or property as a result of such damage) and where the event giving rise to the damage can be said to have taken place in the home country of the corporate defendant. In that case, the victim is presented with the option of choosing the applicability of the law of the home country instead of that of the host country.

Current developments in (prospective) legislation and case law in various EU Member States underline the importance of having a broader possibility to apply home country tort law in foreign direct liability cases brought before EU Member State courts. The solution may lie in an extension of the scope of the Rome II Regulation's special rule on environmental damage to human rights related damage as well as, possibly, health and safety related damage. Many of the policy rationales prompting the introduction of the special rule on environmental damage can be said to also exist – or even more so – with respect to these types of damage if they are caused by the operations of EU-based business enterprises. Extending the scope of the special rule on environmental damage in this way would be crucial to realizing EU (Member States') policies on international corporate social responsibility and business respect for human rights.

Apart from the possibilities that may be offered by (an extended version of) the Regulation's special rule on environmental damage, the application and enforcement through foreign direct liability cases of any legal norms developed in the EU Member States to promote international corporate social responsibility and corporate respect for human rights in host countries, remains dependent on the applicability of one of the Rome II Regulation's other exceptions. The exceptions as regards overriding mandatory provisions of the law of the forum country and as regards the public policy of the forum country could potentially be relevant in this regard. Their role remains limited, however, as these provisions are only to be applied in exceptional circumstances. Furthermore, the potential role in this context of the provision on rules of safety and conduct is also limited, as these rules need only be taken into account by the court as a matter of fact and insofar as the court deems appropriate.

As concerning the issue of applicable law, it is therefore recommended that:

- Future case law by the ECJ and the Member State courts on the application in civil liability cases involving people and planet related harm in non-EU host States as a result of the operations of EU-based internationally operating business enterprises, of the Rome II Regulation's special rule on environmental damage, should be closely monitored.

- Future case law by the ECJ and the Member State courts on the application in civil liability cases involving people and planet related harm in non-EU host States as a result of the operations of EU-based internationally operating business enterprises, of the Rome II Regulation's exceptions on overriding mandatory provisions and public policy and the provision on rules of safety and conduct, should be closely monitored.
- Where necessary, action should be taken at the EU level and/or at the level of the individual Member States to prevent the application of these provisions from hampering the realization of EU (Member States') policies on international corporate social responsibility and business respect for human rights.
- The possibility of extending the scope of the Rome II Regulation's special rule on environmental damage to human rights-related damage as well as, possibly, health and safety related damage should be seriously considered.
- Further research should be conducted into the ways in which such an extension could be formulated so as to promote the realization of EU (Member States') policies on international corporate social responsibility and business respect for human rights.

In foreign direct liability cases brought before EU Member State courts, the issue of procedural rules and practical circumstances is determined by the national procedural rules and litigation practices that are in place in the countries where these cases are brought. According to the UNGPs, states are under an obligation to consider ways to reduce legal, practical and other relevant barriers that could lead to a denial of access to remedies. This is an important provision as, in many of the EU Member States, the pursuit of foreign direct liability cases is likely to be very difficult due to the costs associated with the pursuit of these often complex cases, limited options for pursuing collective actions, and restrictive rules on document disclosure. In combination with the fact that these cases are characterized by the inequality of arms as regards financial scope, level of organization and access to relevant information between the plaintiffs and their corporate opponents, this may render the pursuit of these cases impossible in practice.

This is an issue that needs to be addressed not just at the level of the individual Member States but also at the EU level, if the EU is serious about realizing EU policies or supporting EU Member States' policies on international corporate social responsibility and business respect for human rights. EU involvement in the field of civil procedural law in order to promote private law enforcement of EU norms is not unprecedented in fields such as consumer law and competition law. With this in mind, the reduction of practical and procedural barriers in the EU Member States that may lead to a denial of access to justice before EU Member State courts for victims of corporate human rights and environmental abuse, regardless of the merits of the claims, should be one of the EU's main priorities in the years to come.

As concerning the issue of procedural rules and practical circumstances, it is therefore recommended that:

- Civil liability cases before EU Member State courts involving people and planet related harm in non-EU host states as a result of the operations of EU-based internationally operating business enterprises, should be closely monitored so as to identify any procedural rules or practical circumstances that may lead to a denial of justice for victims of corporate human rights or environmental abuse, regardless of the merits of the claim.
- In doing so, the absence of new or further claims in one or more of the Member States, at a time when the prevalence of this type of litigation is strongly on the increase, should be interpreted as an indication that procedural and practical barriers exist in those Member States that render the pursuit of such claims impossible altogether.
- Where necessary, action should be taken by the individual Member States as well as at the EU level to prevent procedural rules and practical circumstances, especially those relating to costs, collective redress and access to evidence, from resulting in a denial of justice for victims of corporate human rights or environmental abuse.

3 Non-judicial remedies

Company-based grievance mechanisms and international arbitration

Katharina Häusler, Karin Lukas and Julia Planitzer

Case studies: Julia Planitzer, Pablo Paisán Ruiz, Katerina Yiannibas

3.1 Introduction

3.1.1 Context of the research

The possibility for those negatively affected by business activities of using effective remedies through which they can ask for recognition of their grievance and claim compensation, is the litmus test for all business and human rights frameworks.[1] Access to an effective remedy is also a human right itself, enshrined in major international human rights treaties.[2] From a legal perspective, litigation through the courts is the most formal and legally effective avenue, as its outcomes are binding on all parties and, if necessary, enforceable. Court rulings also contribute to providing legal clarity on how to apply human rights norms in the business context and how this corporate responsibility translates into tort law. As the chapter on judicial remedies illustrates, however, formal litigation

1 This chapter was written by Katharina Häusler, Karin Lukas, Julia Planitzer (Ludwig Boltzmann Institute of Human Rights), Pablo Paisán Ruiz (Cuatrecasas, Gonçalves, Pereira), and Katerina Yiannibas (Globernance Institute of Democratic Governance and Assistant Professor of Public and Private International Law at the University of Deusto). The research by the Ludwig Boltzmann Institute of Human Rights has been co-financed in Austria by the Austrian Federal Ministry of Labour, Social Affairs and Consumer Protection (BMASK), and the Chamber of Labour Vienna. The views and opinions expressed in this chapter are those of the authors and do not necessarily reflect the official policy or position of any of the (co-) funding institutions. The Ludwig Boltzmann Institute of Human Rights would like to thank Patrick Harris, Beate Kiewlicz and Niki Koumadoraki for their research and editorial assistance.

2 E.g. Art. 2 International Covenant on Civil and Political Rights; Art. 13 European Convention for the Protection of Human Rights and Fundamental Freedoms; Art. 47 Charter of Fundamental Rights of the European Union.

might be costly, lengthy, difficult or even impossible for various reasons.[3] Therefore, victims' representatives, researchers, but also companies have increasingly been looking into the possibilities of non-judicial remedies in addition or as an alternative to judicial remedies. 'Non-judicial remedies' is, though, a very broad term in itself, encompassing models that are very different in view of their organization and possible outcomes. They can take, for example, the form of state-based or international arbitration, conciliation or mediation (e.g. the OECD Guidelines for Multinational Enterprises with the system of National Contact Points or the World Bank Inspection Panel), sector/industry based initiatives (e.g. the Fair Wear Foundation), or company-based grievance mechanisms.[4] What these mechanisms have in common is that they require the willingness of all actors involved, notably also the business actor, to engage in – to varying degrees – a formalized process. Unlike for court litigation, there exist no formal legal procedures for non-judicial remedies in Europe and the outcome of such procedures can be binding on both parties (either an agreement reached through mediation or a binding decision by an arbitrator), but does not necessarily have to be.

The Framework for Business and Human Rights presented in 2008 by Prof. John Ruggie,[5] Special Representative of the Secretary-General on the issue of human rights and transnational corporations and other business enterprises, builds on three pillars: the state responsibility to protect against human rights abuses by third parties, the responsibility of companies to respect human rights, and the need for an effective access to remedies.[6] Ruggie underlined the significance of effective grievance mechanisms for the 'Protect, Respect and Remedy Framework' to be functional. Norms or corporate codes of conduct will only have a lasting impact if alleged violations of these rules can be investigated and

3 See chapter 1 on Jurisdictional Issues. For an overview, see also: G. Skinner *et al.*, 'The Third Pillar. Access to Judicial Remedies for Human Rights Violations by Transnational Business' 2013. Available at: http://www.biicl.org/documents/182_the_third_pillar.pdf, accessed 13 March 2015.

4 For an overview and analysis of various existing mechanisms, see e.g. C. Rees and D. Vermijs, 'Mapping Grievance Mechanisms in the Business and Human Rights Arena', Corporate Social Responsibility Initiative Report No. 28, Cambridge, MA: John F. Kennedy School of Government, Harvard University, 2008. K. Lukas *et al.*, *Corporate Accountability: The Role and Impact of Non-Judicial Grievance Mechanisms*, Edward Elgar Publishing, 2016 [forthcoming].

5 Prof. Ruggie was appointed SRSG in July 2005, a year after the 'Norms on the Responsibilities of Transnational Corporations and Other Business Enterprises with Regard to Human Rights' drafted by the United Nations' Sub-Commission on the Promotion and Protection of Human Rights between 1999 and 2003, were rejected by the UN Human Rights Commission. The UN Human Rights Council renewed his mandate in June 2008 for a further three years (UN Human Rights Council, Resolution 8/7).

6 UN Human Rights Council, Report of the Special Representative of the Secretary-General on the issue of human rights and transnational corporations and other business enterprises, J. Ruggie, 'Protect, Respect and Remedy: a Framework for Business and Human Rights', A/HRC/8/5, 2008 ('Protect, Respect and Remedy Framework').

those who believe that they have been harmed can seek remediation.[7] While he stressed the importance of national judicial systems, he dedicated much of his further work to developing standards for non-judicial remedies. In 2011, he presented the 'Guiding Principles on Business and Human Rights', which outline the respective duties of states and companies and should help them to implement the 'Protect, Respect and Remedy Framework'.[8] Their endorsement by the UN Human Rights Council in its Resolution 17/4 of 16 June 2011 make the Guiding Principles the most authoritative international framework to date in the area of business and human rights.

Apart from the 'foundational principle' that 'States must take appropriate steps to ensure, through judicial, administrative, legislative or other appropriate means, that when such abuses occur within their territory and/or jurisdiction those affected have access to effective remedy',[9] the Guiding Principles also include 'operational principles' for non-judicial and non-state-based remedies. Based on their responsibility to respect, companies should 'establish or participate in effective operational-level grievance mechanisms for individuals and communities who may be adversely impacted.'[10] However, Ruggie has also highlighted other possible forms of non-judicial remedies, such as industry, multi-stakeholder and other collaborative initiatives. To fulfil the minimum standards of an effective remedy, all forms of non-judicial grievance mechanisms have to follow a set of criteria outlined in the Guiding Principles: they must be legitimate, accessible, predictable, equitable, transparent, rights-compatible, and a source of continuous learning. Company-based, operational-level mechanisms should additionally be based on engagement and dialogue.[11] These criteria are also used for the case studies (see section 3.1.3 Definitions and methodology).

While the Guiding Principles have established themselves as common reference points in the business and human rights discussion, the concept and use of non-judicial remedies – particularly non-state based ones – is contested in academia and civil society. Some authors and civil society organizations have argued that the Guiding Principles were an incomplete framework as some important issues were not adequately addressed and the framework remains vague on effective implementation and access to justice.[12]

7 *Ibid.*, para. 82.

8 UN Human Rights Council, Report of the Special Representative of the Secretary-General on the issue of human rights and transnational corporations and other business enterprises, John Ruggie, 'Guiding Principles on Business and Human Rights: Implementing the United Nations "Protect, Respect and Remedy" Framework', A/HRC/17/31, 2011 ('Guiding Principles').

9 *Ibid.*, para. 25.

10 *Ibid.*, para. 29.

11 *Ibid.*, para. 31.

12 Cf., for example, C. Parker and J. Howe, 'Ruggie's Diplomatic Project and Its Missing Regulatory Infrastructure' in R. Mares (ed), *The UN guiding principles on business and human rights: Foundations and implementation*, Leiden, Boston, Martinus Nijhoff, 2012; Human Rights Watch, 'UN Human Rights Council: Weak Stance on Business Standards.

Operational-level grievance mechanisms – the 'company-created human rights remedy mechanisms' recommended by Ruggie – are on the rise. However, such mechanisms also entail serious risks for rights-holders and also for the right to remedy in general.[13] Consequently, mechanisms should be based on a partnership between a company and primary stakeholders, including those potentially affected by a company's activities.[14] As a potential alternative model, an international NGO is currently developing a community-driven operational grievance mechanism, which should be designed primarily by the affected populations themselves to meet their needs and expectations.[15]

3.1.2 *Research interest*

Analyzing and evaluating all forms of non-judicial remedies would go far beyond the scope of this work. Building on previous research in this area, we thus focus on company-based (operational-level) grievance mechanisms.[16] While there is already extensive literature and research on some international or state-based non-judicial remedies, such as the OECD Guidelines for Multinational Enterprises and its system of National Contact Points or the World Bank Inspection Panel,[17] there is still little knowledge about the functioning of company-based grievance mechanisms. As the UN Working Group on the issue of human rights

Global Rules Needed, Not Just Guidance', statement of 16 June 2011, available at https://www.hrw.org/news/2011/06/16/un-human-rights-council-weak-stance-business-standards, accessed 29 March 2016.

13 It is shown that, for example, potential users of the grievance mechanisms fear retaliation, see Access, *ACCESS to Remedy in Context of Business and Human Rights: Improving the Effectiveness of Non-Judicial Grievance Mechanisms*, (Expert meeting report, 3–4 April 2014), p. 10, available at http://accessfacility.org/sites/default/files/Report%20Expert%20Meeting%20on%20Grievance%20Mechanisms_ACCESS%20Facility_The%20Hague_%203-4%20April%202014_0.pdf, accessed 3 November 2016. A further example, as described in one case, is the inclusion in the grievance mechanism of a provision that required beneficiaries of remedies to sign legal waivers concerning future legal actions: see J. Kaufman and K. McDonnell, 'Community-Driven Operational Grievance Mechanisms', 1(1) *Business and Human Rights Journal* (2016) 129.

14 S. Knuckey and E. Jenkin, 'Company-created remedy mechanism for serious human rights abuses: a promising new frontier for the right to remedy', 19(6) *The International Journal of Human Rights* (2015) 801–827.

15 For details on this project see: http://www.earthrights.org/legal/community-driven-ogms, accessed 07 April 2016; J. Kaufman and K. McDonnell, 'Community-Driven Operational Grievance Mechanisms', 1(1) *Business and Human Rights Journal* (2016) 127–132.

16 On the terminology, see *infra* 'Definitions and methodology'.

17 Cf., for example, K. Lukas, 'The Inspection Panel of the World Bank. An Effective Extra-judicial Complaint Mechanism?' in Jan Wouters *et al.*, 'Improving Delivery in Development: The Role of Voice, Social Contract, and Accountability', 6 *The World Bank Legal Review* (2015) Washington, DC, World Bank; J. W. Ramsing *et al.*, 'Remedy Remains Rare. An analysis of 15 years of NCP cases and their contribution to improve access to remedy for victims of corporate misconduct', OECD Watch, 2015, available at http://www.oecdwatch.org/publications-en/Publication_4201/@@download/fullfile/Remedy%20Remains%20Rare.pdf, accessed 20 May 2016.

and transnational corporations and other business enterprises noted in its report to the UN General Assembly in 2015, '[r]esearch in the field of business and human rights lacks comprehensive data on the number and nature of complaints against companies for their adverse impacts and the effectiveness of the bodies tasked with investigating and remediating those impacts'.[18]

Most companies have only started to develop such mechanisms during the last decade – often as part of their work to implement the Guiding Principles, or as part of their wider corporate social responsibility or business and human rights policy and/or their membership in the UN Global Compact.[19] Furthermore, so far studies have mostly analyzed company-based grievance mechanisms of US-based companies, which already have a longer history of use.[20]

In line with the topic of the overall research project, this chapter analyses grievance mechanisms established by European-based companies (one headquartered in the EU and one in Norway). Bearing in mind the limited scope of this research project, this work is not able to provide a full picture of the set-up and implementation of company-based grievance mechanisms in Europe. Rather we would like to use the example of two big companies operating in different sectors to illustrate the possible potentials and challenges of such mechanisms. By distilling good practices of and challenges for company-based grievance mechanisms, we aim to contribute to a better understanding of the functioning of these mechanisms among European stakeholders. The research outlined below should provide examples and support other companies when developing their own grievance mechanisms. We would also like to highlight the kind of grievances for which company-based mechanisms can be a useful (often easier and quicker) alternative or supplement to litigation and where, in our view, formal judicial procedures need to step in. The baseline for assessing the appropriateness of company-based grievance mechanisms is the understanding that, from a human rights perspective, out-of-court mechanisms are clearly inappropriate where violations reach the level of serious crime. In cases where national judicial systems entirely fail to provide any access to remedy (e.g. due to an ongoing conflict situation in the country) it can be still reflected, if operational-level grievance mechanisms could nevertheless be used in such cases as a first step for ensuring recognition and first remediation for those affected.

In comparison to the non-judicial company-based grievance mechanisms, this chapter also analyzes international arbitration under the auspices of the

18 United Nations General Assembly, 'Report of the Working Group on the issue of human rights and transnational corporations and other business enterprises.' (A/70/216, 30 July 2015), para. 88, available at http://www.un.org/en/ga/search/view_doc.asp?symbol=A/70/216, accessed 22 April 2016.

19 The 'Communication on Progress' participants have to submit annually includes also a sub-criterion 'Operational-level grievance mechanisms for those potentially impacted by the company's activities (BRE 4 + ARE 4)' in the self-assessment form. (https://www.unglobalcompact.org/docs/communication_on_progress/GC_Advanced_COP_selfassessment.pdf, accessed 16 March 2015).

20 Cf., for example, B. Linder et al., *The Right to Remedy: Extrajudicial Complaint Mechanisms for Resolving Conflicts of Interest between Business Actors and Those Affected by their Operations,* Ludwig Boltzmann Institute of Human Rights, 2013; C. Rees and D. Vermijs, *op. cit.*

Permanent Court of Arbitration at The Hague (PCA) as an example of how and under what conditions international arbitration could potentially be adapted to provide a remedy for human rights grievances, in addition to non-judicial grievance mechanisms. The potential use of international arbitration for promoting access to remedy for victims of business-related human rights abuses has gained increasing relevance in recent years. The chapter explores what possibilities international arbitration at the PCA could offer for companies and affected individuals and, on the other hand, what issues and challenges the arbitration mechanism could present.

3.1.3 Definitions and methodology

This chapter takes a comparative approach to two company-based grievance mechanisms and arbitration under the auspices of the PCA. In the literature, there exist various definitions of non-judicial remedies operating at company level and some also distinguish between 'complaints' and 'grievances'. For the purpose of the research on the two company-based mechanisms, we use the Guiding Principles' broad definition of 'operational-level grievance mechanism' as a basis, while using 'operational-level' and 'company-based' interchangeably:

> Operational-level grievance mechanisms are accessible directly to individuals and communities who may be adversely impacted by a business enterprise. They are typically administered by enterprises, alone or in collaboration with others, including relevant stakeholders. They may also be provided through recourse to a mutually acceptable external expert or body. They do not require that those bringing a complaint first access other means of recourse. They can engage the business enterprise directly in assessing the issues and seeking remediation of any harm.[21]

Our research focused deliberately on a small number of mechanisms to allow in-depth research within the limited resources available. The companies whose grievance mechanisms are analyzed in the case studies were selected on the following basis:

- European context: the companies are headquartered in a Member State of the EU or the European Free Trade Association.
- Relevance of companies: the companies chosen for the case studies are multinational enterprises, which are well known in public. They represent different industry sectors and have the potential to act as role models within their sectors.
- Human rights relevance: the selected grievance mechanisms refer to procedural and material human rights requirements (mentioning, at least

21 UN Human Rights Council, Guiding Principles, *op. cit.* para. 29.

implicitly, international standards and documents) and conform prima facie to the minimum criteria for non-judicial remedies.

- Length of operation: the selected grievance mechanisms have already been working for some years, to allow evaluation of their outcomes.

The project builds on desk research of relevant international standards and documents, academic literature, company documents, and empirical data and information gained through expert interviews. It uses the international human rights framework as its legal basis for assessment. The effectiveness of the mechanisms – also in terms of human rights compatibility – is assessed based on the criteria established by the Guiding Principles.[22] According to these criteria, non-judicial mechanisms must be:[23]

(a) legitimate: enabling trust from the stakeholder groups for whose use they are intended, and being accountable for the fair conduct of grievance processes including the question whether; the mechanism, in its work, is sufficiently independent from the management.
(b) accessible: being known to all stakeholder groups for whose use they are intended, and providing adequate assistance for those who may face particular barriers to access;
(c) predictable: providing a clear and known procedure with an indicative time frame for each stage, and clarity on the types of process and outcome available and means of monitoring implementation;
(d) equitable: seeking to ensure that aggrieved parties have reasonable access to sources of information, advice and expertise necessary to engage in a grievance process on fair, informed and respectful terms;
(e) transparent: keeping parties to a grievance informed about its progress, and providing sufficient information about the mechanism's performance to build confidence in its effectiveness and meet any public interest at stake;

22 UN Human Rights Council, Guiding Principles, *op. cit.* para. 31.
After having tested the effectiveness criteria of the Guiding Principles in four pilot projects on company/stakeholder grievance mechanisms, Prof. Ruggie suggested a slightly adapted set of criteria: UN Human Rights Council, Report of the Special Representative of the Secretary-General on the issue of human rights and transnational corporations and other business enterprises, John Ruggie, Addendum, *Piloting principles for effective company/stakeholder grievance mechanisms: A report of lessons learned*, A/HRC/17/31/Add.1, 2011.

23 Based on the Guiding Principles' criteria, CSR Europe – a business network for corporate social responsibility – has developed process requirements for effective company grievance mechanisms, which can serve as a useful 'checklist' for companies, which are setting up new mechanisms: CSR Europe, *Assessing the effectiveness of company grievance mechanisms. CSR Europe's Management of Complaints Assessment (MOC-A) Results*, 2013, available at: http://www.csreurope.org/sites/default/files/Assessing%20the%20effectiveness%20of%20Company%20Grievance%20Mechanisms%20-%20CSR%20Europe%20(2013)_0.pdf, accessed 30 May 2016.

(f) rights-compatible: ensuring that outcomes and remedies accord with internationally recognised human rights;
(g) a source of continuous learning: drawing on relevant measures to identify lessons for improving the mechanism and preventing future grievances and harms.

Operational-level mechanisms should also be:

(h) based on engagement and dialogue: consulting the stakeholder groups for whose use they are intended in their design and performance, and focusing on dialogue as the means to address and resolve grievances.

Research shows that, in general, 'there is not a one-size-fits-all approach'[24] for grievance mechanisms. However, it is recommended that conflicts be settled as far as possible at local level.[25] The effectiveness of the mechanisms can also include further – more specific – criteria. For example, a previous study analyzed the victim's perspective on case outcomes. It showed that the majority of victims would not be satisfied with the outcome experienced. An element identified to improve the outcome is the integration of a neutral convener or facilitator in the process, who is acceptable to all stakeholders and helps to equalize power imbalances among stakeholders.[26] Generally, there are – due to various reasons – limited data available to assess the effectiveness of company-based grievance mechanisms. Non-judicial mechanisms typically do not follow up after an agreement on whether the grievance was resolved fairly and what impact the agreement had.[27]

For the case studies, each of the researchers has conducted at least two interviews, with company representatives, union representatives, arbitrators, or representatives of victims having used the mechanism (at least one with a company representative and one with an external stakeholder). In total, the research team conducted eight interviews, either personally, via phone or via IP telephony.[28]

Researchers encountered various difficulties in accessing information about grievance mechanisms and finding stakeholders willing to give an interview. The identified gap of data concerning the number and nature of grievances against companies and related remedial action[29] could be confirmed in the course of this

24 Van Genugten *et al.*, *Company-community Conflicts: The Effectiveness of Outcomes of Non-judicial Conflict Resolution. An Explanatory Report.* Report prepared for ACCESS Facility, The Hague (2013, copy with authors), p. 56.
25 *Ibid.*
26 *Ibid.*, pp. 37–39.
27 Access, *ACCESS to Remedy in Context of Business and Human Rights: Improving the Effectiveness of Non-Judicial Grievance Mechanisms*, (Expert meeting report, 3–4 April 2014), p. 11.
28 See the list of interviewees in Annex. For confidentiality reasons a number of interviews have been anonymised.
29 Cf. the Statement by M. Jungk, UN Working Group on the issue of human rights and transnational corporations and other business enterprises at the 70th session of the General

research. While many European companies report to have established operational level grievance mechanisms,[30] concrete information about their operation is challenging to access. Therefore, a number of companies, which were initially preselected for possible analysis of their grievance mechanisms, could finally not be considered for a case study due to a lack of information.[31]

3.2 Case studies on company-based grievance mechanisms

3.2.1 Siemens AG (case study by Julia Planitzer)

3.2.1.1 General description of the company and its grievance mechanism

Siemens consists of Siemens AG, a stock corporation under the federal laws of Germany, and a total of about 800 legal entities, including minority investments. Siemens' headquarters is situated in Munich.[32] In 2014, Siemens restructured its organization and its operations are grouped into seven sub-groups: Power and Gas, Wind Power and Renewables, Energy Management, Building Technologies, Mobility, Digital Factory, Process Industries, and Drives. In addition, there are segments on Healthcare, and Financial Services.[33] As of 30 September 2015, Siemens had 348,000 employees worldwide;[34] around 60 per cent of all employees work in Europe, Central Asia, Africa, and the Middle East. Seventy thousand employees work in the Americas.[35]

Since 2003, Siemens has been a participant to the UN Global Compact and describes its commitment to the Compact's ten principles in, for instance, a report dedicated to sustainability.[36] The Communication on Progress 2015 indicates that Siemens reports on an operational-level grievance mechanism 'for

Assembly, Third Committee, Item 72 (b&c), 27 October 2015, http://www.ohchr.org/EN/NewsEvents/Pages/DisplayNews.aspx?NewsID=16660&LangID=E, accessed 23 March 2016.

30 Cf. the 'Communications on progress' in the framework of the Global Compact initiative (https://www.unglobalcompact.org/what-is-gc/participants).

31 Researchers conducted initial research on fourteen European companies (including the two companies finally selected).

32 Siemens, *Annual Report 2014, Financial Report – Combined Management Report*, p. 172.

33 *Ibid.*, p. 172, 174; Siemens, *Annual Report 2015* (*A. Combined Management Report*), p. 2.

34 Siemens, *Annual Report 2015* (*A. Combined Management Report*), p. 2.

35 As of 30 September 2014, see Siemens, *Siemens at a glance – Fiscal 2014* for the time period between May 2014 and May 2015, p. 6, http://www.siemens.com/annual/14/en/download/pdf/Siemens_AR2014_At-a-glance.pdf, accessed 28 October 2015.

36 Siemens, *Sustainability Information 2015 as addendum to the Siemens Annual Report*, p. 36, http://www.siemens.com/about/sustainability/pool/en/current-reporting/siemens_sustainability_information2015.pdf, accessed 09 December 2015.

those potentially impacted by the company's activities'.[37] Additionally, reporting follows the Sustainability Reporting Guidelines of the Global Reporting Initiative (GRI)[38] and recommendations of Transparency International.[39]

The 'Siemens Business Conduct Guidelines' cover areas such as Siemens' core values. The section on treatment of business partners and third parties lays out Siemens' principles concerning anti-corruption and working with suppliers. In addition, the guidelines comprise regulations concerning the protection of information and concerning environment, safety and health. A fundamental principle for Siemens AG and its subsidiaries is observing the law and the legal system in every country of business. The company does not tolerate discrimination, which covers internal cooperation as well as cooperation with external partners.[40] Suppliers are supposed to share Siemens' values and therefore should 'respect basic human rights of employees' and 'comply with laws prohibiting child labor'.[41]

Siemens developed a specific code of conduct for suppliers and third party intermediaries. Suppliers are expected to respect fundamental employment rights as set out in the core treaties of the UN and ILO and the document also refers to the OECD Guidelines and the UN Global Compact. Suppliers should ensure they pay fair remuneration and minimum wages and safeguard the right of workers to form trade unions. Furthermore, the supplier is expected to ensure that employees can lodge complaints with superiors without fear of reprisal.[42] The web-based training for suppliers also stresses by referring to the ILO the prohibition of employment of children under fifteen years old.[43] Suppliers are also requested to support the implementation of the code of conduct in their own supply chains.[44] Additionally, Siemens advises suppliers to implement human rights. This also includes, as pointed out in a toolkit for suppliers on how to implement human rights practices in their companies, the establishment of grievance mechanisms that allow the filing of complaints in a safe and anonymous

37 UN Global Compact, Communication on Progress 2015, https://www.unglobalcompact.org/participation/report/cop/create-and-submit/advanced/145241, accessed 18 November 2015.
38 See, for an overview, Siemens GRI G4 Index 2015: http://www.siemens.com/about/sustainability/pool/en/current-reporting/siemens_gri_g4-index-2015_comprehensive-option.pdf, accessed 09 December 2015.
39 Siemens, *Sustainability Information 2015 as addendum to the Siemens Annual Report*, p. 10.
40 Siemens (Corporate Compliance Office), *Siemens Business Conduct Guidelines* (January 2009), A.1 and A.2.
41 *Ibid.*, B.8.
42 Siemens, *Sustainability in the Supply Chain – Code of conduct for Suppliers and Third Party Intermediaries*, Version 3.0, 2015–07, p. 12.
43 Siemens, *Sustainability in the Supply Chain, Web-based training (Code of Conduct for Siemens Suppliers, Child Labor)*, https://wbt.siemens.com/static_wbts/wbtesscsup/player.htm, accessed 25 May 2016.
44 Siemens, *Annual Report 2014*, Corporate Governance, B.3.3., p. 139.

environment.[45] The toolkit for suppliers recommends establishing adequate processes and initiatives and indicates that suppliers that are advanced in terms of human rights should implement grievance mechanisms.[46] The code of conduct for suppliers should go beyond the first tier of suppliers and should also be applied by the suppliers of the suppliers.[47]

In order to identify potential risks of e.g. human rights abuses or corruption among the around 90,000 suppliers of Siemens, it established a risk-based system of appropriate processes. This system comprises not only sustainability self-assessments by suppliers but also risk evaluations conducted by the Siemens' purchasing department, supplier quality audits and sustainability audits conducted by external auditors. The procedures of supplier quality audits were amended and include sustainability questions; in the fiscal year 2015 Siemens conducted, in total, 981 supplier quality audits. Suppliers conducted 3,508 self-assessments and, in the fiscal year 2015, Siemens commissioned 50 external audits, mostly conducted in Asia and Australia. External audits are the strongest tool among the audits to review the performance of suppliers[48] and the number of these audits is expected to increase significantly in 2016.[49] In case the audits show deviations from the Siemens requirements, suppliers have to implement improvement measures within a reasonable period. These actions are, among others, monitored by follow-up audits conducted by external auditors. In 2015, in total, 35 measures to ensure the prohibition of child labour had to be implemented by suppliers. Measures concerning the respect for the basic human rights of employees were requested by Siemens 357 times. Measures for health and safety of employees (388) rank highest.[50] Measures to ensure that no children are working in the company mostly concern proper mechanisms to prevent child labour by suppliers. Furthermore, companies, for instance, have to show how they monitor working time in order to be able to document extra hours correctly. Suppliers were requested to implement attendance recording systems. Cooperation with five suppliers was finally stopped since emergency exits were not accessible for workers.[51]

In order to ensure compliance with the Siemens Business Conduct Guidelines and its code of conduct for suppliers and third party intermediaries, Siemens installed several channels of reporting. Generally, employees can file complaints

45 Cf. Siemens, *Supply Chain Management, Toolkit on Implementing Human Rights*, http://w5.siemens.com/cms/supply-chain-management/en/sustainability/toolkit/implement/human-rights/pages/home.aspx, accessed 25 May 2016.

46 *Ibid.*

47 Siemens, *Sustainability in the Supply Chain – Code of conduct for Suppliers and Third Party Intermediaries*, Version 3.0, 2015–07, p. 24.

48 Siemens, *Sustainability Information 2015 as addendum to the Siemens Annual Report*, p. 19.

49 INT 2, representative of Siemens AG/Supply Chain Management, 03 December 2015.

50 Siemens, *Sustainability Information 2015 as addendum to the Siemens Annual Report*, p. 18–19.

51 INT 2, representative of Siemens AG/Supply Chain Management, 03 December 2015.

internally with their supervisor, compliance officer, or internal works council. In addition, internal and external stakeholders can use two secure reporting channels: the compliance hotline called 'Tell Us' and the Siemens' ombudsperson.[52] The system of reporting is embedded in Siemens' compliance system which consists of three segments: (1) Prevent: by implementing training and policies; (2) Detect: by installing reporting channels; and (3) Respond: by implementing consequences for misconduct.[53]

The hotline 'Tell Us' functions via telephone and internet and allows the filing of reports anonymously. The website clearly indicates that the application is not part of the Siemens websites or the Siemens intranet.[54] Users can select a country and a language (thirteen languages are available), and telephone and website are accessible 24/7.[55] The second channel is an external ombudsperson. The ombudsperson is an attorney based in Munich whose contact details are published online and in the relevant reports.[56] In the fiscal year 2015, further inquiries and investigations were conducted in 568 cases, which were reported via the hotline, the ombudsperson, and via notifying the supervisors. These reported compliance cases led to 208 disciplinary sanctions, including warnings and dismissals.[57]

In 2012, Siemens, the central works council of Siemens, the German Industrial Union of Metal workers (IG Metall) and the IndustriAll Global Union signed an International Framework Agreement (IFA).[58] The agreement refers to Siemens' membership in the UN Global Compact and to its commitment to fundamental labour rights defined by international conventions. The agreement fleshes out core principles such as prohibition of child labour, freedom of association, and the right to collective bargaining and appropriate remuneration. In addition, the role of suppliers is mentioned and that Siemens actively endeavours to have these principles incorporated in the policies of its suppliers.[59] Having a look at various IFAs, it can be shown that the majority of IFAs' provisions concern the suppliers' obligation to implement the provisions themselves. Formulations concerning the degree to which they are binding vary among

52 Siemens (Corporate Compliance Office), *Siemens Business Conduct Guidelines* (January 2009), G, p. 24; Siemens, *Sustainability in the Supply Chain – Code of conduct for Suppliers and Third Party Intermediaries*, Version 3.0, 2015–07, p. 38.

53 Siemens, *Annual Report 2014*, Corporate Governance, B.3.3., p. 138.

54 Cf. https://www.bkms-system.net/bkwebanon/report/clientInfo?cin=19siem14, accessed 09 December 2015.

55 Siemens, Compliance Hotline Tell Us, http://www.siemens.com/about/sustainability/en/core-topics/compliance/system/tell-us.htm, accessed 09 December 2015.

56 Siemens, Ombudsman, http://www.siemens.com/about/sustainability/en/core-topics/compliance/system/ombudsman.htm, accessed 29 October 2015.

57 Siemens, *Sustainability Information 2015 as addendum to the Siemens Annual Report*, p. 29.

58 See for the English version of the agreement: http://www.industriall-union.org/sites/default/files/uploads/documents/siemens-gfa-2012-english_final.pdf, accessed 29 October 2015.

59 See sections 2.3, 2.4, 2.5 and 2.9 of the IFA.

IFAs.[60] The wording used in the IFA of Siemens concerning suppliers can be categorized as encouraging the latter to implement the IFA principles, by referring to the code of conduct for suppliers, but does not create a responsibility of Siemens to have the IFA implemented in the whole supply chain. In addition to the protection of labour rights, the IFA should support the development of structures representing the interests of Siemens employees at national level and strengthen networking of these structures at international level. In order to reach this goal, regular meetings at regional level are foreseen.[61]

The central works council negotiating team (*Verhandlungsdelegation*) together with the IG Metall are in charge of monitoring and supporting the implementation of the agreement. About every two months, the central works council negotiating team meets with the IG Metall and the Siemens management for relevant matters.[62] However, primarily, IFA should be implemented by regional structures of workers' interest representation.[63] Implementation of the IFA is ongoing. The first steps included awareness raising for the IFA at regional level by conducting meetings of representatives of employees of all Siemens facilities in China, by organizing special training series (e.g. in India), and translating the IFA into eleven languages. A further step was the establishment of sustainable structures for communication for matters of the IFA.[64]

The IFA refers to 'internal and local/national complaint and arbitration facilities' that all employees or representatives should turn to in case of grievances. Internal complaint facilities should be used primarily. Possible breaches of the agreement can be submitted via the company's internal communication channels, such as the 'Tell Us' hotline. The central works council negotiating team has to deal only with complaints that cannot be solved through the local and national complaint and arbitration facilities. The team should 'prevent external legal disputes'.[65] Therefore, the central works council negotiating team can be seen as the highest instance for more serious complaints in order to solve complaints internally.[66]

The IFA or the Siemens Business Conduct Guidelines describe a company-based grievance mechanism by referring to the 'Tell Us' hotline and the external ombudsperson. Available material though does not indicate that concerning Siemens' actions or actions of joint ventures, in which Siemens is involved, such formal grievance mechanisms are used in relation to alleged human rights abuses

60 K. Lukas, *Labour Rights and Global Production* (2013) Vienna, Graz, NWV, 153.

61 IG Metall (eds.), *Arbeitnehmervertretung bei Siemens in China, Erfolgreiche Chinesisch-Deutsche Kooperation* (2015) 8.

62 INT 1, representative of IG Metall, 02 November 2015.

63 IG Metall (eds.), *Arbeitnehmervertretung bei Siemens in China, Erfolgreiche Chinesisch-Deutsche Kooperation* (2015) 8–9.

64 *Ibid.*, p. 9.

65 See sections 2.10.2, 2.10.4 and 2.10.5 of the International Agreement.

66 INT 1, representative of IG Metall, 02 November 2015.

caused by activities related to Siemens. Siemens is, for example, involved through the joint venture Voith Hydro in the construction of the Belo Monte Dam in Brazil. As addressed by several NGOs to the management at the Annual Shareholders' Meetings in 2015 and 2016,[67] the Belo Monte Dam violates, inter alia, indigenous land rights, cultural rights, and the right to life, food, and health. The NGOs Gegenstroemung, Amazon Watch, and International Rivers recommended Siemens to conduct an independent audit and implement in the future a complaint mechanism 'accessible to threatened and/or affected local communities in project areas'.[68] Similarly, Siemens is involved in the construction of the Agua Zarca Hydroelectric Dam on the Gualcarque River in Honduras through the joint venture Voith Hydro. Demonstrations against the project led to death threats, violence, and police harassment against the indigenous Lenca families in the region.[69] Siemens holds a minority of Voith Hydro (35 per cent) and claims that Siemens itself would not be part of the consortium that is in charge of this project.[70] After several submissions and initiatives of NGOs informing Siemens about the situation in Honduras,[71] Voith Hydro decided to

67 Siemens, *Shareholder Counterproposals and Election Nominations for the Annual Shareholders' Meeting 2015 of Siemens AG* on January 27th 2015, http://www.siemens.com/investor/pool/en/investor_relations/events/annual_shareholders_meeting/2015/Gegenantraege_en_20150113.pdf, accessed 02 December 2015; Siemens, *Shareholder Counterproposals and Election Nominations for the Annual Shareholders' Meeting 2016 of Siemens AG* on January 26th 2016; see the counterproposal of the Association of Ethical Shareholders, pp. 3–4, http://www.siemens.com/investor/pool/de/investor_relations/events/hauptversammlung/2016/Gegenantraege_de_20160112.pdf, accessed 02 February 2016.

68 Letter of Gegenstroemung, Amazon Watch and International Rivers addressed to Siemens CEO Joe Kaeser, dated 20 January 2015, http://amazonwatch.org/assets/files/2015-belo-monte-siemens-hr-dossier.pdf, accessed 17 May 2017.

69 Letter of International Rivers, Friends of the Earth International, *Oekunemisches Buero fuer Frieden und Gerechtigkeit* addressed to Siemens CEO Joe Kaeser, dated 20 January 2015, http://amazonwatch.org/assets/files/2015-agua-zarca-siemens-hr-dossier.pdf, accessed 02 December 2015; and speech of Andrea Lammers (*Ökumenisches Büro für Frieden und Gerechtigkeit*) at the Annual Shareholders' Meeting 2016 of Siemens AG on January 26th 2016, http://www.kritischeaktionaere.de/fileadmin/Dokumente/Reden_2016/Rede_Andrea_Lammers_Siemens_HV_2016.pdf, accessed 02 February 2016. In early March 2016, Berta Cáceres, Honduran human rights defender of the Lenca community and central figure in the protests against the Agua Zarca dam project, was assassinated in her house. The organization International Rivers immediately started an online calling on the builders of the dam, including Siemens, to terminate their investment or work concerning the dam. See http://org.salsalabs.com/o/2486/p/dia/action3/common/public/?action_KEY=19314, accessed 21 March 2016.

70 Letter of Siemens AG, dated 09 March 2016, available at http://business-humanrights.org/sites/default/files/documents/Statement%20der%20Siemens%20AG%2009032016.pdf; and statement of Siemens reacting to the assassination of Berta Cáceres, 09 March 2016, available at http://business-humanrights.org/en/honduras-second-member-of-indigenous-group-murdered-within-2-weeks-dutch-development-bank-suspends-activity#c133990, last accessed 23 March 2016.

71 Speech of Andrea Lammers (*Ökumenisches Büro für Frieden und Gerechtigkeit*) and of Christian Russau (*Dachverband der Kritischen Aktionärinnen und Aktionäre*/German umbrella association of critical shareholders) at the Annual Shareholders' Meeting 2016

stop working on this project until further notice. Voith's decision is supported by Siemens.[72] Additionally, Siemens receives criticism for its involvement in Morocco's programmes for renewable energy in the Western Sahara. Siemens has been commissioned to supply turbines and engineering consulting support by the Moroccan financial group Nareva Holding for wind farms in the Western Sahara that have a negative impact on the people living in the area, related in particular to issues connected to unclear land ownership[73]

3.2.1.2 Evaluation of the mechanism along the established criteria

LEGITIMACY

Both communication channels for possible breaches of rules set out in, for instance, the International Framework Agreement (IFA) or the code of conduct for suppliers, are organized externally. The hotline 'Tell Us' is operated by an external company and the ombudsperson is an independently organized external attorney. The follow-up actions after filing reports are clearly internally organized. The Siemens' compliance system deals with the reports starting with an assessment followed by a four stage compliance investigation.[74]

The IFA, on the other hand, describes a different procedure for reports. While also using the 'Tell Us' hotline, the central works council negotiating team is tasked with handling grave breaches that cannot be resolved by national or local mechanisms. The procedure between filing a report and the work of

of Siemens AG on January 26th 2016, http://www.kritischeaktionaere.de/fileadmin/Dokumente/Reden_2016/Rede_Andrea_Lammers_Siemens_HV_2016.pdf, accessed 02 February 2016.

72 Cf. *Sueddeutsche Zeitung*, *Wasserkraft-Projekt gestoppt*, (C. Giesen, 05 May 2016, http://www.sueddeutsche.de/wirtschaft/voith-hydro-wasserkraft-projekt-gestoppt-1.2981466, accessed 17 May 2016) and Stuttgarter-Zeitung. de, *Umstrittenes Wasserkraftwerk – Voith Hydro legt Honduras-Projekt auf Eis*, (T. Magenheim, 05 May 2016, http://www.stuttgarter-zeitung.de/inhalt.umstrittenes-wasserkraftwerk-voith-hydro-legt-honduras-projekt-auf-eis.ce60efae-14ca-4e85-8f8f-aed05d5e159c.html, accessed 17 May 2016).

73 Western Sahara Resource Watch, *Dirty Green March – Morocco's controversial renewable energy projects in occupied Western Sahara*, WSRW Report August 2013, pp. 12–13. Also the UN Security Council discussed the matter of contracts with foreign companies in Western Sahara. The UN Under-Secretary-General for Legal Affairs issued a legal opinion on the matter of contracts of the Moroccan authorities with foreign companies for the exploration of mineral resources in Western Sahara and held that these contracts are not illegal per se. The opinion, however, states, that 'if further exploration and exploitation activities were to proceed in disregard of the interests and wishes of the people of Western Sahara, they would be in violation of the principles of international law applicable to mineral resource activities in Non-Self-Governing Territories,' UN Security Council, letter dated 29 January 2002 from the Under-Secretary-General for Legal Affairs, the Legal Counsel, addressed to the President of the Security Council, S/2002/161 (12 February 2002), para. 25.

74 Siemens, *Annual Report 2014*, Corporate Governance, B.3.5., p. 140 *et seq.*

the special group is not further described in the IFA. However, the central works council negotiating team consists of five works council representatives,[75] which shows a higher degree of independence from the management than the regular compliance procedure.

In general, the procedure of filing complaints as described in the IFA is still in its initial phase and establishing a practical process for solving issues between employees' representatives and the management is identified as a future challenge.[76] Currently, it is not clear whether the central works council negotiating team has to deal formally with a complaint, since this team discusses complaints, which could not be solved by negotiations between, for example, the works council and management first.[77] For all possible channels to file complaints, the follow-up procedure is not clearly defined, or is internally organized without explaining to what extent all stakeholders involved can have an influence on the process itself. In the case of IFA, external monitoring is to a certain extent conducted through the involvement of works council representatives. Based on the available material and information it is challenging to assess the extent to which comprehensive procedural mechanisms that ensure fair conduct of the processes are in place.

ACCESSIBILITY

The possibility of using the hotline is mentioned in various relevant documents, which are distributed to the relevant internal and external stakeholders. However, documents such as the code of conduct may not reach employees at every level worldwide. Although it is mentioned that reporting led to 653 further inquiries in 2014,[78] there is no further information given on how many of those were initiated by reports via the hotline, besides using other reporting channels (ombudsperson or supervisors).

The accessibility of the ombudsperson seems to be lower since it is not explained when and under which circumstances the ombudsperson should be contacted rather than the hotline. It seems that the ombudsperson is intended to be installed for grave possible breaches. Clearer guidance and, for example, a form for reporting might have an encouraging impact on employees.

The IFA also mentions the hotline as a possibility for reporting violations of employees' rights. However, in practice, the role of the hotline concerning matters of labour rights violations seems to be rather limited. Rather, informal networks and personal contacts help to make the trade union IG Metall aware of possible cases of labour rights violations. However, as indicated by a

75 INT 1, representative of IG Metall, 02 November 2015.

76 IG Metall (eds.) *Arbeitnehmervertretung bei Siemens in China, Erfolgreiche Chinesisch-Deutsche Kooperation* (2015) 9.

77 INT 1, representative of IG Metall, 02 November 2015.

78 Siemens, *Annual Report 2014*, Corporate Governance, B.3.5., p. 140.

representative of IG Metall, the trade union is notified about approximately two possible cases of violation of workers' rights per year, but is not being made aware of all cases. For example, IG Metall was informed about labour rights violations at a Siemens plant in Indonesia concerning obligatory breaks for workers and usage of restrooms.[79] The development of regional structures for labour rights representation is therefore crucial in order to raise awareness about the possibility of complaining within the framework of the IFA.

For suppliers, Siemens recommends installation of a company-based grievance mechanism, but it is not a mandatory requirement. However, Siemens requires suppliers to have a form of labour rights representation. Suppliers should have, for instance, a workers' council to ensure a form of complaints mechanism. In case there are no internal grievance mechanisms, the Siemens structures, including the hotline, should apply. It is important for Siemens to ensure dissemination about these measures; suppliers can implement several measures, such as making the hotline better known in the company, having a letterbox for anonymous complaints, or by having a designated ombudsperson within the supplier.[80]

Assessments concerning the predictability, equitability, transparency and rights-compatibility of the grievance mechanism are challenging to make, since information concerning the grievance mechanisms can be found in different frameworks of the company, for instance, the supply chain management and IFA. A comprehensive structure for grievance mechanisms for human rights abuses is required from suppliers and relates to, for example, payment of minimum wages, compliance with maximum working hours, or preventing child labour. The IFA itself, for example, does not define the forms of remediation or how those could be assessed. Time frames seem to be undetermined and information about remedies achieved is limited.

DIALOGUE AND ENGAGEMENT, CONTINUOUS LEARNING

The possibility to lodge complaints as described in the IFA is based on discussions of the Siemens management on the one side and the works council as well as the trade union IG Metall on the other. In order to further enhance the process of complaints lodging, regional structures should be developed. Regional or country-based interest representatives should raise awareness among employees about lodging complaints. Meetings in different countries such as China, United States, and South Korea are conducted regularly. For example, after a two-year process of negotiations and training, several trade union representatives of Siemens plants in China are now able to exchange and interact in a national coordination forum.[81] Hence, dialogue plays a central role in the complaints mechanism as described in the IFA. Continuous learning plays also

79 INT 1, representative of IG Metall, 02 November 2015.
80 INT 2, representative of Siemens AG/Supply Chain Management, 03 December 2015.
81 INT 1, representative of IG Metall, 02 November 2015.

a vital role within the supply chain management. Siemens organizes workshops and training for suppliers and offers brochures in order to support the implementation of the code of conduct.[82] Furthermore, Siemens' buyers play an important role and are regularly in touch with the suppliers concerning their efforts in reaching the required standards.[83] For this, it is beneficial that Siemens usually has a subsidiary in the country concerned.[84] Furthermore, sustainability forms an integral part within the buyers' training programme.[85] If a supplier does not fulfil the required standards, the responsible procurement department defines follow-up actions with the supplier.[86]

3.2.1.3 Concluding remarks

The UN Global Compact reporting tool 'Communication on Progress' indicates that Siemens uses a grievance mechanism. The existing internal grievance mechanisms, consisting of the hotline and the ombudsperson, are framed under compliance[87] and are to a large extent focused on efforts against corruption. The International Framework Agreement (IFA) describes a grievance mechanism for violation of labour rights, including the use of internal complaint facilities. These mechanisms also apply to the supply chain. Reporting channels for complaints are clearly defined and also requested from suppliers. In case there is a violation taking place at a supplier's company, procedures exist by which Siemens ensures that the supplier fulfils Siemens's requirements.[88]

The IFA was signed in 2013 and has since been implemented. Nevertheless, a procedure for complaints of violations of labour laws still needs to be further developed. Although there is a rather informal means of lodging complaints to the trade union, this system might require further institutionalization. Part of the process – by designating the central works council negotiating team as the highest instance for serious violations – is defined in the IFA, but seems unused thus far for specific cases. The works council negotiating team and the trade union IG Metall are currently paving the way to realizing the procedure of complaints lodging in the future. As a prerequisite, interested unions at regional level are needed to represent the rights of Siemens employees and support the lodging of complaints.

82 Siemens, *Sustainability in the Supply Chain – Code of conduct for Suppliers and Third Party Intermediaries*, Version 3.0, 2015–07, p. 36.

83 *Ibid.*

84 INT 2, representative of Siemens AG/Supply Chain Management, 03 December 2015.

85 Siemens, *Sustainability Information 2015 as addendum to the Siemens Annual Report*, p. 19.

86 *Ibid.*

87 See, for instance, the Siemens GRI G4 Index 2015, showing the 'Human Rights Grievance Mechanisms' are dealt with as part of the Siemens compliance grievance mechanisms, pp. 6–7, http://www.siemens.com/about/sustainability/pool/en/current-reporting/siemens_gri_g4-index-2015_comprehensive-option.pdf, accessed 09 December 2015.

88 INT 2, representative of Siemens AG/Supply Chain Management, 03 December 2015.

Additionally, the IFA primarily focuses on abuses of labour rights in its company and subsidiaries worldwide. That the mechanisms of IFA should also cover the situation of workers in suppliers of Siemens is seen as challenging. However, workers' councils of Siemens plants in the country should tackle this issue and assess the situation of labour rights in suppliers.[89] Efforts channelled to Siemens' subsidiaries primarily concern the implementation of the IFA. Grievance mechanisms for workers in the supply chain form part of the Siemens' supply chain management. The hotline is mentioned as a possibility for workers of the supply chain. In addition, it is seen as beneficial that Siemens usually has a subsidiary in the country and therefore can react quickly in the case of complaints about possible violations of standards. The role of Siemens' local buyers is stressed as highly important. In addition to the different audit procedures, Siemens representatives can visit – unannounced – suppliers and assess the situation.[90]

In general, two frameworks for reporting and grievance mechanisms can be identified: one framework is embedded in the Siemens' compliance mechanisms and includes the 'Tell Us' hotline and the ombudsperson; the second framework is the procedure described in the IFA. The first is primarily seen as an instrument of compliance rather than a fully-fledged grievance mechanism according to the UN Guiding Principles. The procedure described in the IFA is indeed understood clearly as a grievance mechanism, but still seems to be in an earlier stage of its full implementation. For both frameworks, clear procedures and time frames for grievance for human rights abuses are available only to a limited extent. Both frameworks are also applicable to the supply chain. Grievance mechanisms described in different frameworks and the supply chain use the same entry channel. Efforts within the Siemens' supply chain management and the implementation of IFA by the workers' council and trade unions concerning this matter might be further harmonized and possible interactions between different strands of grievances within Siemens might be further strengthened.

3.2.2 Statoil (case study by Pablo Paisán Ruiz)

3.2.2.1 General description of the company and its grievance mechanism

Statoil ASA ('Statoil') is a Norwegian oil company that was founded on 14 June 1972 by the Norwegian Parliament (in its origins it was a state-owned company) and was established with the objective of creating a national player with enough resources for competing with foreign oil and gas extraction companies. Statoil discovered its first oil and gas deposit in 1976, creating its first offshore extraction platform ten years later.

89 INT 1, representative of IG Metall, 02 November 2015.
90 INT 2, representative of Siemens AG/Supply Chain Management, 03 December 2015.

In the oil and gas sector in general, operational activities can have varied social and environmental impacts,[91] and can give rise to grievances[92] because of human rights abuses.

In 2001, the Norwegian Parliament approved the listing of Statoil's shares on the Oslo Stock Exchange and on the New York Stock Exchange.[93] The consequence of Statoil's shares being listed on an official secondary securities market is that Statoil must comply with the legislation applicable to companies listed in both countries (Norway and the US). It must also follow 'mandatory disclosure' or explain why it does not follow the respective corporate governance guidelines (under the 'comply or explain' principle) since investors expect that listed companies not only comply with certain financial standards but also follow certain practices aimed at maintaining appropriate standards of corporate responsibility, integrity, and accountability to shareholders.[94]

The current version of the Norwegian Code of Practice for Corporate Governance, which dates from 30 October 2014, establishes that the core concept of corporate social responsibility is the company's responsibility for the manner in which its activities affect people, society and the environment, and it typically addresses human rights; prevention of corruption; employee's rights, health and safety; the working environment; discrimination, and environmental issues, in line with G20/OECD Principles of Corporate Governance (2015).[95] The latter establish that in addition to their commercial objectives, companies are encouraged to disclose policies and performance relating to business ethics, the environment and, where material to the company, social issues, human rights, and other public policy commitments. Such information may be important for certain investors and other stakeholders to better evaluate the relationship between companies and the communities in which they operate and the steps that companies have taken to implement their objectives.

91 Statoil, "Sustainability Report 2014", p. 10. The report states that 'Statoil acknowledges the scientific consensus on human-induced climate change and supports the efforts of the United Nations and its member states to agree and implement necessary measures to prevent dangerous manmade interference with the climate system'.

92 UN Human Rights Council, Guiding Principles, *op. cit.* para. 25, offering a definition of grievance in its commentary by explaining that 'grievance is understood to be a perceived injustice evoking an individual's or a group's sense of entitlement, which may be based on law, contract, explicit or implicit promises, customary practice, or general notions of fairness of aggrieved communities'.

93 Statoil, *Annual Report 2014*, p. 14, http://www.statoil.com/no/InvestorCentre/AnnualReport/AnnualReport2014/Documents/DownloadCentreFiles/01_KeyDownloads/20-F_2014.pdf, accessed 29 March 2016.

94 For an overview see also H. Christiansen and A. Kolderstrova *The Role of Stock Exchanges in Corporate Governance* (2009). Available at: http://www.oecd.org/finance/financial-markets/43169104.pdf, accessed 17 May 2016.

95 OECD, *G20/OECD Principles of Corporate Governance – OECD Report to G20 Finance Ministers and Central Bank Governors* (2015), https://www.oecd.org/daf/ca/Corporate-Governance-Principles-ENG.pdf, accessed 29 March 2016.

Corporate governance includes, in particular, initiatives with the objective to achieve smart, sustainable, and inclusive growth by encouraging proper interaction between companies, their shareholders and other stakeholders and extending the reporting requirements with regard to non-financial parameters establishing a more comprehensive risk profile of the company, enabling more effective design of strategies to address those risks. Sustainability implies that the company must effectively manage the governance, social, and environmental aspects of its activities as well as financial operations.[96]

As a result of the foregoing, since 2001 Statoil publishes an annual sustainability report separately from the financial statements. In its first sustainability report for the fiscal year 2001, Statoil makes an express reference to the respect of human rights in developing countries and focuses on observing and promoting fundamental standards for human rights since some of the world's petroleum is found in zones of instability and conflict.

In 2012, Statoil and other oil companies made large offshore gas discoveries in Tanzanian territorial waters. A pipeline transporting natural gas from a region in Tanzania to Dar es Salaam led to demonstrations, since the people living in this region wanted the gas to be kept in the region. The demonstrations are seen as being beyond the direct responsibility of Statoil, 'but shows that Statoil can be vulnerable to the expectations of impoverished groups'.[97] As a reaction, Statoil acted locally: it avoided seismic shooting at night, so that Statoil did not risk colliding with local fishing boats. Statoil hired local employees. However, the Tanzanian authorities showed little effort to resolve these issues by consulting civil society.[98] In the context of the Tanzania's Liquefied National Gas (LNG) project,[99] Statoil is one of the partners. The government acquired land and the implementation of the project will lead to relocations and compensation on land rights. It would seem vital that Statoil should strengthen its role in the implementation by using the grievance mechanism established and ensuring informed consent by the communities concerned.[100] The most recent Statoil sustainability reports of 2014 and 2015 contain a specific section on 'Human Rights', in which the creation of a Human Rights Steering Committee was cited as an objective. This committee was established in January 2015 and it comprises senior representatives from key business areas and staff functions and is chaired

96 International Corporate Governance Network, *ICGN Global Governance Principles 2014*, http://www.ecgi.org/codes/documents/icgn_global_governance_principles_2014_en.pdf, accessed 29 March 2016.

97 Pål Wilter Skedsmo *et al.* (Fridtjof Nansen Institute), *Doing good by doing well? – Statoil in Sub-Saharan Africa* (2013), p. 27, https://www.fni.no/getfile.php/132230/Filer/Publikasjoner/Doing_good_by_doing_well.pdf, accessed 29 March 2016.

98 *Ibid.*, pp. 26–27.

99 See for further information on the LNG project, R. Denny, *Accountability through active citizenship: improving Petroleum Governance in Ghana, Mozambique and Tanzania, Baseline Survey Report – Tanzania*, p. 12.

100 INT 2, representative of NGO, 7 April 2016.

by a Statoil chief compliance officer. This group advises on policy and implementation matters and received training on the UN Guiding Principles. It is not a grievance mechanism but if there are any severe cases of human rights issues or violations, they will be notified to the Human Rights Steering Committee.[101] In 2015, Statoil developed a stand-alone human rights policy after consultation with stakeholders, union representatives and international experts on human rights, consistent with the UN Guiding Principles on Business and Human Rights.[102] Statoil's board of directors approved it on 10 September 2015.[103] According to this policy, Statoil commits to treating those working for the company and those impacted by its operations, fairly and without discrimination. It also commits to providing appropriate remediation, including, where relevant, effective grievance mechanisms in the location where it may have caused or contributed to adverse human rights impacts.

Due to Statoil's policy commitment to respect human rights, the company strives to conduct its business operations consistently with the UN Guiding Principles on Business and Human Rights and the OECD Guidelines for Multinational Enterprises, according to its sustainability report.[104] The origin of grievance mechanisms at Statoil was an internal labour issue. The use of the grievance mechanisms to remedy abuses of human rights related to environmental issues, however, did not become widespread until the year 2011. Statoil was also confronted with complaints under the OECD Guidelines' National Contact Points procedure in recent years, relating to environmental concerns and the consultation of local communities.[105]

101 Statoil, *Sustainability Report 2015*, p. 33, http://www.statoil.com/no/InvestorCentre/AnnualReport/AnnualReport2015/Documents/DownloadCentreFiles/01_KeyDownloads/2015_Sustainability_report.pdf, accessed 29 March 2016.

102 *Ibid.*

103 Statoil, *Human Rights Policy (Final Version adopted by the Board of Directors on 10 September 2015*, http://www.statoil.com/en/EnvironmentSociety/Sustainability/Downloads/Human%20Rights%20Policy.pdf, accessed 17 May 2016.

104 Statoil, *Sustainability Report 2014*, p. 31. As briefly mentioned above, the OECD Guidelines are a set of recommendations of the governments of Member States to companies operating in and from their territory with voluntary principles and standards to guide companies in their international operations. The UN Guiding Principles on Business and Human Rights promote the use, value, and power of effective community grievance mechanisms.

105 For instance, a complaint concerning the Corrib gas project in North West County Mayo (Ireland) run by a consortium of Shell, Statoil, and Vermilion. Initially, the Irish National Contact Point was dealing with this case, but later the Dutch National Contact Point was asked to deal with it, since Shell, having its seat in the Netherlands, was also involved. Pobal Chill Chomáin (People of Kilcommon) and two supporting non-governmental organizations ('Action from Ireland' and 'Sherpa') filed on 21 August 2008 a complaint concerning the Corrib gas project. There were no options for the resolution of the dispute through mediation and the National Contact Points from Ireland and The Netherlands issued a statement with remarks and recommendations. According to the statement, when an EU company in its exercise of due diligence is faced with concerns of local

Statoil expects its suppliers to respect human rights and apply Statoil's ethical requirements.[106] According to the Statoil Supplier Declaration,[107] Statoil's suppliers have to ensure that all suppliers' employees have access to effective grievance mechanisms.

Community queries are addressed by regular contact with the communities and by compliance with any formal grievance-handling procedures required by the regulatory authorities (e.g. concerning labour law).[108]

For the above-mentioned purposes, Statoil participates (being a founding member) in IPIECA. IPIECA is an association of the oil and gas sector established in 1974 (after the creation of the United Nations Environment Program (UNEP)), specializing in environmental and social issues. By means of its working groups managed by members and through its executive management, IPIECA combines the knowledge and experience of oil and gas companies and associations, which represent more than half of the oil production in the world.

Although the origins of the IPIECA lie in the search for solutions to the challenges of climate change, at the dawn of the twenty-first century, its activity extends to community grievance mechanisms and, in January 2015, it approved a manual for implementing operational-level grievance mechanisms.[109]

---

stakeholders over their situation and rights, it has the responsibility to consider, where appropriate, going beyond what is legally required when it comes to holding consultations with the local community. See http://www.oecdwatch.org/cases/Case_150, accessed 11 April 2016.

In a different case, the Norwegian Climate Network and Concerned Scientists Norway filed on 28 November 2011 a complaint against Statoil alleging that Statoil breached the environment chapter of the OECD Guidelines by investing in the oil sands of Alberta and thereby contributing to Canada's violation of international obligations to reduce greenhouse gas (GHG) emissions in the period from 2008 to 2012, not considering relevant international agreements when Statoil began its activities in Canada. This complaint was rejected in March 2012 because it did not meet the criteria specified in the OECD Procedural Guidelines and it was directed towards national policies rather than company policies. In fact, the complaint was filed against a company but aimed to influence law-making policies in Canada and Norway. See on this case http://nettsteder.regjeringen.no/ansvarlignaringsliv-en/files/2013/12/statoil_first.pdf, accessed 11 April 2016; http://www.oecdwatch.org/cases/Case_248?set_language=en, accessed 11 April 2016; and http://www.oecd.org/daf/inv/mne/StatoilAssessmentandConclusion.pdf, accessed 11 April 2016.

106 Statoil, *Sustainability Report 2015*, p. 33.

107 Statoil, *Supplier Declaration* (COM140295_1_ REV. 1), http://www.statoil.com/en/OurOperations/Procurement/Downloads/Supplier%20Declaration%20Aug2014.pdf, accessed 28 May 2016.

108 Statoil, *Sustainability Report 2014*, p. 31; Statoil, *Sustainability Report 2015*, p. 33.

109 IPIECA, *Community grievance mechanisms in the oil and gas industry – A manual for implementing operational-level grievance mechanisms and designing corporate frameworks* (2015), p. 6, http://www.ipieca.org/publication/community-grievance-mechanisms-oil-and-gas-industry-manual-implementing-operational-leve, accessed 29 March 2016.

In 2014, Statoil developed a framework for site-level community grievance mechanisms.[110] They are separate from any workforce grievance mechanism following the UN Guiding Principles[111] and have been implemented so far for the Statoil operations in Brazil, Tanzania, and the US.[112] Furthermore, Statoil has contributed to the IPIECA grievance mechanisms guide.[113]

During the years 2014 and 2015, Statoil received and mediated one grievance in Tanzania related to exploration activities. Statoil carried out seven field visits when implementing the grievance mechanism. In 2015 no grievance was received in Brazil; however, three field visits were carried out to listen to local fishermen and to promote awareness about the grievance mechanism.[114]

The community grievance mechanism of Statoil is a site-level mechanism,[115] which encompasses also, for instance, community liaison officers.[116] Statoil ensures accessibility by providing multiple points of access: through Statoil personnel acting locally, through a local telephone number available for complaints in each project, and through the internet. Until 2015, only a few reports under the community grievance mechanism were lodged in Tanzania. Cases concerned reduced fish catch and compensation for nets cut by company vessels.[117] However, how effectively the grievance mechanism will work when the intensity of Statoil's operations increase will need to be assessed in the future. Currently, Statoil has not yet started producing in Tanzania.[118]

Statoil also provides to all individuals free access by phone or the internet to Statoil's Ethics Helpline, which is available in English and local languages in all countries where Statoil operates. Through this helpline, any possible breaches of the company's code of conduct or applicable laws and regulations, as well as concerns related to Statoil's health, safety and environment responsibilities, and internationally recognized human rights, can be reported.[119] When a claim is raised, a report number is assigned and the claimant will be given a personal

110 Statoil, *Annual Report 2014*, p. 31.

111 IPIECA, *Community grievance mechanisms in the oil and gas industry – A manual for implementing operational-level grievance mechanisms and designing corporate frameworks*, 2015, p. 6, http://www.ipieca.org/publication/community-grievance-mechanisms-oil-and-gas-industry-manual-implementing-operational-leve, accessed 29 March 2016.

112 Statoil, *Annual Report 2014*, p. 6; Statoil, *Annual Report 2015*, p. 34.

113 IPIECA, *Community Grievance Mechanisms toolbox*, 2014, http://www.ipieca.org/publication/community-grievance-mechanism-toolbox, accessed 29 March 2016.

114 Statoil, *Annual Report 2015*, p. 34.

115 Statoil, *Annual Report 2014*, p. 31.

116 R. Denny, *Accountability through active citizenship: improving petroleum governance in Ghana, Mozambique and Tanzania – Baseline Survey Report*, January 2015, p. 19, http://www.oxfamamerica.org/static/media/files/NORAD_Tanzania_Baseline_Report_1.pdf, accessed 25 March 2016.

117 *Ibid.*, p. 19.

118 *Ibid.*; and INT 2, representative of NGO, 07 April 2016.

119 Statoil's Ethics Helpline, http://www.statoil.com/en/about/ethicsvalues/pages/etikkhjelpelinjen.aspx, accessed 17 May 2016.

identification number (PIN) in order to follow up and check on the status of the claim.

3.2.2.2 Evaluation of the mechanism along the established criteria

LEGITIMACY

Statoil's internal grievance processes have been used for complaints of groups of individuals.[120] Additionally, Statoil has also been involved in non-judicial proceedings under the OECD Guidelines for Multinational Enterprises.[121]

The grievance mechanism established by Statoil is established internally, including all possibilities for having access to the mechanism. However, there are multiple points of access, including through Statoil's local team. This is important, since people possibly affected at places where Statoil operates might have no access to the internet. When implementing the grievance mechanism at the local level in Tanzania (2014–2015), seven field visits were carried out by company representatives to hear the concerns of communities.[122]

It is indicated that Statoil is responding quickly to requests from civil society. Compared to other oil companies that are working in Tanzania, Statoil seems to make greater efforts in terms of engagement with civil society.[123] Although cooperation with NGOs exists, further strengthening the inclusion of external partners, such as NGOs, as an access point for grievances would be recommended. Issues such as confidentiality have to be ensured in order to establish trust in the procedure.

This is also strongly linked to the equitability of the process. An equitable grievance mechanism includes the possibility for affected stakeholders to have access to information provided by an organization or group that is organized externally of the company.

ACCESSIBILITY AND PREDICTABILITY

All stakeholders, regardless of their location, have access to the Statoil grievance mechanism. In 2014, a corporate framework for a site-level grievance mechanism was established, setting itself up in Brazil, Tanzania and the US.[124] The mechanism is based on the local context and available in local languages. So far, few

120 Statoil, *Sustainability Report 2015*, p. 34.
121 See concerning the OECD Guidelines for Multinational Enterprises: http://www.oecd.org/daf/inv/mne/48004323.pdf, accessed 17 May 2016.
122 Statoil, *Sustainability Report 2015*, p. 34.
123 INT 2, representative of NGO, 07 April 2016.
124 Statoil, *Sustainability Report 2014*, p. 31.

complaints have been filed, the reason for which could be the short time of existence of the mechanism and the fact that potentially more sensitive onshore operations in Tanzania have not fully started yet. However, for the future, it will be important to monitor the use of complaint mechanisms, as a lack of cases might also be a sign of a lack of awareness of the mechanisms, or a lack of trust in the process.

Statoil has had complaints from Tanzanian fishermen due to Statoil's exploration activities in Tanzania. The grievance mechanism for these complaints has been implemented locally by the Statoil team in Tanzania, resolving the complaints by means of economic compensation, which has been considered adequate in order to repair the damage caused.[125] Concerning predictability, it is not possible to assess the indicative time frame due to the limited number of cases dealt with in the grievance mechanism. However, it has been shown that, in the context of Tanzania, Statoil generally seems to react swiftly to requests from civil society.[126]

TRANSPARENCY

The mechanism is very young. Regarding the cases mediated so far, accessible information about the procedures and outcomes is limited. Therefore, it would be recommended that further information be provided in the sustainability reports on current experiences, which would also improve predictability for those considering using the mechanism. Furthermore, the process including envisaged time frames should be described in more detail.

3.2.2.3 Concluding remarks

The oil and gas sector in which Statoil operates potentially affects human rights abuses in many fields, impacting on employees, local communities, or the environment. The companies that operate in this sector are mainly large companies whose shares are listed on the stock exchange markets (and, thus, with great visibility). The exploration activities are sometimes executed in countries with a rather weak human rights record, due to a lack of governance structures and weak rule of law.

The combination of both factors means that the stakeholders of these companies demand that the companies take a step forward in terms of environmental and social responsibility and, in sum, on human rights issues. The awareness of these concerns is shown in the sustainability reports of these

125 Statoil, *Annual Report 2015*, p. 34.
126 INT 2, representative of NGO, 07 April 2016.

companies,[127] including Statoil. Although reports of these companies show increased awareness for human rights matters, it seems that there is still a difference between the day-to-day activities with potential impact on human rights, and their reports.

The grievance mechanism is an excellent tool for approaching both the text and the reality and Statoil is taking a determined step forward in applying community grievance mechanisms for human rights abuses. Nevertheless, we are at the 'beginning of the road' as the culture on grievance mechanisms for human rights abuses is relatively new in large companies. It is clear that effective grievance mechanisms should be part of oil and gas sector companies to address human rights issues in their operations.

An effective community grievance mechanism in the oil and gas sector is a key tool to solve issues in a non-judicial, effective and rapid manner (however, it neither replaces nor impedes access to the judicial system). This mechanism is a process for receiving, investigating, responding to or mediating complaints or grievances from affected communities in a timely, fair and consistent manner.[128]

However, the effectiveness of the grievance mechanisms established in Brazil and Tanzania is challenging to assess, since the mechanisms have only been in place since 2014. Furthermore, in the context of Tanzania, Statoil's activities are limited at the moment, but will increase in future. It has to be tested in the future, when the number of grievances might rise, to see how effectively the mechanism works. It is recommended that more information be published concerning the procedure of the mechanism, the involvement of civil society and local communities, and issues raised in the framework of Statoil's field visits.

127 According to Repsol's corporate responsibility report for 2014, it has several channels which the stakeholders can use to report or process grievances with respect to any aspect of its operations and as part of its overriding pledge to upholding human rights. Repsol has committed, within the realm of its human rights due diligence efforts, to establishing effective communication and grievance mechanisms at the operations level, see Repsol, *Corporate Social Responsibility Report 2014*, pp. 137, 138, https://www.unglobalcompact.org/system/attachments/cop_2015/200651/original/RSC_Report_2014_eng.pdf?1445872937, accessed 17 May 2016; and according to BP's sustainability report for 2014, BP works with IPIECA to develop tools for managing community grievances, see BP, *Sustainability Report 2014*, p. 50, http://www.bp.com/content/dam/bp/pdf/sustainability/group-reports/Sustainability_Report_2014.pdf, accessed 17 May 2016.

128 IPIECA, *Community grievance mechanisms in the oil and gas industry – A manual for implementing operational-level grievance mechanisms and designing corporate frameworks* (2015) p. 6, http://www.ipieca.org/publication/community-grievance-mechanisms-oil-and-gas-industry-manual-implementing-operational-leve, accessed 29 March 2016.

3.3 Case study on the potential of the arbitration mechanism: Permanent Court of Arbitration (case study by Katerina Yiannibas)[129]

3.3.1 *General description and functioning of the permanent Court of Arbitration*

The Permanent Court of Arbitration (PCA) is an intergovernmental organization established in 1899 at The Hague through the adoption of the Convention for the Pacific Settlement of International Disputes at the first International Peace Conference. The PCA was established by the Contracting States to facilitate arbitration and other forms of dispute resolution so as to ensure the pacific settlement of international differences.[130] While the PCA was initially conceived to handle interstate disputes, the PCA has evolved to provide access to an international remedy for non-state parties. The PCA's basic organizational structure is outlined in its two founding documents: the aforementioned 1899 Convention and its revision in 1907. As of May 2016, the PCA has 119 Member States that have acceded to one or both of the founding conventions.[131]

Despite the nomenclature, the PCA is not a typical court; rather, it administers and facilitates arbitration, conciliation and fact-finding. In terms of organizational structure, the PCA comprises a panel of arbitrators named the Members of the Court, the Administrative Council, and its Secretariat, the International Bureau. The Members of the Court are potential arbitrators that are named by Member States for a term of six years, with the possibility of renewal, based on their known competency in international law and moral reputation.[132] The Administrative Council, comprising Member States' diplomatic representatives accredited to the Netherlands and chaired by the Netherlands Minister of Foreign Affairs, provides general guidance and supervises the PCA's administration, budget and expenditure.[133] The permanent Secretariat of the PCA, known as the International Bureau, is headed by its Secretary-General and is composed of a multinational and multilingual legal and administrative staff that administer arbitration,

129 The author would like to thank Brooks W. Daly (Permanent Court of Arbitration), Lise Johnson (Columbia Center for Sustainable Investment) and Denis Bensaude (Bensaude-Paris) for their invaluable insights as well as Prof. Marta Requejo Isidro (Max Planck Institute Luxembourg) and Prof. Nerea Magallon Elosegui (University of Deusto) for their constructive review.

130 Hague Convention for the Pacific Settlement of International Disputes 1899, Art. 1. The 1899 Convention was revised at the Second Peace Conference at The Hague in 1907.

131 Permanent Court of Arbitration Member States, https://pca-cpa.org/en/about/introduction/member-states/, accessed 11 March 2016.

132 PCA Members of the Court-Panel of Arbitrators, https://pca-cpa.org/en/about/structure/members-of-the-court/, accessed 11 March 2016.

133 PCA Administrative Council, https://pca-cpa.org/en/about/structure/administrative-council/, accessed 11 March 2016.

conciliation and fact-finding disputes between any combination of states, private parties, state-controlled entities, and intergovernmental organizations.[134]

The PCA is headquartered in The Hague at the Peace Palace, home also to the International Court of Justice – the principal judicial organ of the United Nations. Cases under the auspices of the PCA can be administered at the Peace Palace or, alternatively, at any location as agreed by the parties or directed by the arbitral tribunal. While the working languages of the PCA are English and French, parties may agree to conduct proceedings in any language.[135]

The PCA provides various arbitration services if so agreed by the parties, which could be implemented at a cost. Under Article 6 of the 2010 United Nations Commission on International Trade Law (UNCITRAL) Arbitration Rules, the Secretary-General of the PCA can designate or act as an appointing authority for the selection of arbitrators. In such cases, the Secretary-General retains the discretion to appoint the most appropriate candidate as arbitrator and is not restricted by the list of arbitrators that make up the Members of the Court. The International Bureau can further provide registry services and administrative support to the parties and the arbitrators, including financial administration, logistical and technical support for meetings and hearings, travel arrangements, and general secretarial and linguistic support.[136] In practice, arbitrator fees are not usually set by the PCA but rather reached by agreement between the parties. In 1995, the PCA established the Financial Assistance Fund with the objective of helping developing states with the costs of international dispute resolution administered by the PCA. The fund consists of voluntary financial contributions by states, intergovernmental organizations, national institutions, as well as natural and legal persons, and is available to qualifying states or state controlled entities, with the approval of an external and independent Board of Trustees.[137]

As concerning PCA procedure in the conduct of international arbitration, there is no one single set of procedural rules. The PCA has developed a number of sets of arbitration rules,[138] based largely on texts of UNCITRAL that parties

134 PCA Services, https://pca-cpa.org/en/services/, accessed 11 March 2016.

135 *Ibid.*

136 PCA Arbitration Services, https://pca-cpa.org/en/services/arbitration-services/, accessed 11 March 2016.

137 PCA Financial Assistance Fund for Settlement of International Disputes, Terms of Reference and Guidelines (as approved by the Administrative Council on December 11, 1995), Arts 4–5.

138 Rules include: Permanent Court of Arbitration (PCA) Arbitration Rules 2012; PCA Optional Rules for Arbitrating Disputes between Two States; PCA Optional Rules for Arbitrating Disputes between Two Parties of Which Only One Is a State; PCA Optional Rules for Arbitration Involving International Organizations and States; PCA Optional Rules for Arbitration between International Organizations and Private Parties; PCA Optional Rules for Arbitration of Disputes Relating to Natural Resources and the Environment; PCA Optional Rules for Arbitration of Disputes Relating to Outer Space Activities.

may choose depending on the nature and circumstances of the dispute, although the PCA often administrates cases under the conduct of UNCITRAL Arbitration Rules or other ad hoc rules.[139] In 2001, the PCA adopted a set of comprehensive environmentally tailored procedural rules: Optional Rules for Arbitration of Disputes Relating to the Environment and/or Natural Resources.[140] In addition to the adoption of the environmental rules, the PCA maintains a list of specialized arbitrators for environmental disputes as well as scientific and technical experts for potential appointment as expert witnesses. As part of their work in the field of dispute avoidance and settlement concerning environmental issues, the PCA and the United Nations Environment Programme (UNEP) convened a working group in 2006. The working group developed a set of guidelines; including 'ways of increasing access to justice on environmental matters, inter alia, through public interest lawsuits to apply and implement environmental laws, the use of preliminary remedies in environmental disputes, and the use of environmental expertise in dispute settlement concerning environmental issues.'[141] A question emerges of whether similar rules and guidelines could be adopted by the PCA in the field of business and human rights.

Since its inception in 1899, the PCA has managed several hundred cases, including cases in which the PCA was asked to provide full administrative support as well as cases where the PCA was asked to appoint or constitute the arbitral tribunal or to decide on the removal of an arbitrator.[142] The large majority of the PCA caseload has come about in the last thirty years, in part due to the notable increase in bilateral investment treaties in the 1990s as well as being the result of a general trend reflecting a global increase in dispute settlement through arbitration.[143] In 2015, the PCA administered 135 cases, of which 76 were investor state arbitrations arising under bilateral or multilateral investment treaties and national investment laws; 44 arbitrations arising under contracts involving a state, intergovernmental organization, or other public entity; eight interstate arbitrations; one arbitration under the PCA Optional Rules for Arbitration of Disputes Relating to Natural Resources and/or the Environment; and one conciliation between a private party and an intergovernmental organization arising under a contract submitted to conciliation in accordance with the

139 United Nations Conference on Trade and Development (UNCTAD), *Dispute Settlement*, Module 1.3: Permanent Court of Arbitration, 2003, p. 11. Available at: http://unctad.org/es/Docs/edmmisc232add26_en.pdf, accessed 27 May 2015.

140 For full text of the PCA Environmental Rules, see https://pca-cpa.org/wp-content/uploads/sites/175/2016/01/Optional-Rules-for-Arbitration-of-Disputes-Relating-to-the-Environment-and_or-Natural-Resources.pdf, accessed 11 March 2016.

141 UNEP/PCA Advisory Group on Dispute Avoidance and Settlement concerning Environmental Issues, Working Group Report, 2–3 November 2006, p. 1.

142 Interview with Brooks W. Daly, 24 June 2015.

143 Hugo Siblesz, Secretary-General PCA, *What Role for the Permanent Court of Arbitration Today?* Remarks, New York University School of Law, 11 February 2013.

UNCITRAL Conciliation Rules (1980).[144] Of these, approximately 10 per cent of cases have a human rights component,[145] and approximately 20 per cent of cases deal with the activities of EU corporations in non-EU countries.[146]

3.3.2 *Evaluation of the mechanism along the established criteria*

3.3.2.1 *Legitimacy*

The principal concerns over legitimacy[147] in international arbitration centre on the resolution of public law issues through a private adjudication system[148] and the accountability of arbitrators.[149] Civil society has expressed a certain scepticism about arbitration as a conflict resolution mechanism when the dispute involves aspects of public law and policy, including human rights.[150] Whether national courts will recognize the arbitrability of human rights issues, i.e. the capability of settlement of human rights issues by arbitration, depends largely on substantive domestic law on arbitration, which can vary significantly between jurisdictions and could result in the non-enforcement of an arbitral award.[151]

In commercial cases, a noted advantage of international arbitration is the finality and non-appealable nature of the award. These principles, intended to avoid unnecessary delays and to combat the obstruction of process by dilatory or recalcitrant parties, have come under scrutiny in cases with a noted public interest, particularly in cases with a human rights component.[152] Appellate

144 PCA Annual Report 2015. Available at https://pca-cpa.org/wp-content/uploads/sites/175/2016/02/PCA-annual-report-2015.pdf, accessed 11 March 2016.

145 See also J. Levine, 'The interaction of international investment arbitration and the rights of indigenous peoples' in *Investment Law within International Law*, ed. Freya Baetens, (2013) Cambridge University Press: Cambridge, 108.

146 Interview with Brooks W. Daly, 24 June 2015.

147 UN Human Rights Council, Guiding Principles on Business and Human Rights: Implementing the United Nations 'Protect, Respect and Remedy' Framework (UN Guiding Principles 2011), 2011, para. 31a. Legitimacy is defined as 'enabling trust from the stakeholder groups for whose use they are intended, and being accountable for the fair conduct of grievance processes'.

148 See D. Behn, 'Legitimacy, Evolution and Growth in Investment Treaty Arbitration: Empirically evaluating the State-of-the-Art', 46(2) *Georgetown Journal of International Law* (2015) 367.

149 Interview with Denis Bensaude, 03 March 2016.

150 Interview with Lise Johnson, 03 March 2016. There are also extensive debates about this question in academia; see e.g. Pierre-Marie Dupuy, Ernst-Ulrich Petersmann, and Francesco Francioni (eds). *Human Rights in International Investment Law and Arbitration* (2009) Oxford: Oxford University Press.

151 See C. Pamboukis, 'On Arbitrability: The Arbitrator as a Problem Solver' in *Arbitrability: International & Comparative Perspectives*, (eds. Loukas A. Mistelis and Stavros L. Brekoulakis) (2009) Wolters Kluwer: The Netherlands.

152 See *AT&T Mobility v Concepcion*, 563 U.S. 333 (2011). (As concerning the principle of finality in regards to collective consumer redress, the court reasoned: 'We find it hard to believe that defendants would bet the company with no effective means of review, and even harder to believe that Congress would have intended to allow state courts to force such a decision.')

review was originally contemplated at the 1899 founding convention of the PCA at The Hague, but was not made part of the default arbitration mechanism. This does however leave it open to the parties to agree to appellate review. So far, no cases submitted to the PCA have made this part of the procedural regime. There are no rules, however, that would exclude appellate review.[153]

There are further concerns relating to the accountability of arbitrators. There is no international qualification for arbitrators. Moreover, the parties appoint the arbitrators, an element of the arbitration mechanism that raises concerns of impartiality and independence. Specifically, the concern relates to the conflict of interest inherent in counsel acting as arbitrator in other cases.[154] The selection of arbitrators by the parties does, however, provide an opportunity to select an adjudicator with a high level of expertise and specialization in international human rights.[155] The work to identify those most qualified and with an established reputation for impartiality is work that could be done by the PCA, as it has previously done in cases relating to the environment and/or natural resources and outer space. The PCA Member States have twice adopted procedural rules that have been targeted at specific sectors: PCA Optional Rules for Arbitration of Disputes Relating to the Environment and/or Natural Resources; PCA Optional Rules for Arbitration of Disputes Relating to Outer Space Activities. In both cases the Member States decided that the subject matter had a strong public interest. Should PCA Member States decide that it is appropriate, they could in turn give a mandate to the PCA to prepare procedural rules arising in disputes relating to corporate related human rights abuses, as well as to develop a specialized panel of arbitrators and experts.[156] This would provide a reference for parties to choose arbitrators among this group of identified experts in international human rights law. The accountability of arbitrators also relates closely to the issues of costs and transparency; both will be discussed in the sections below.

153 In 2013, the American Arbitration Association (AAA) and the International Centre for Dispute Resolution (ICDR) adopted Optional Appellate Arbitration Rules.

154 See M. Solanes and A. Jouravlev, Revisiting Privatization, Foreign Investment, International Arbitration and Water, Santiago: CEPAL, 2007.

155 Interview with Brooks W. Daly, 24 June 2015.

156 PCA, *PCA Responds to Queries on Arbitral Legitimacy*, available at: http://archive.pca-cpa.org/shownews67ec.html?ac=view&pag_id=1261&nws_id=414, accessed 11 March 2016. In response to a 2014 inquiry on arbitral legitimacy by the International Congress and Convention Association, the PCA responded that it was the institution's role to foster legitimacy and to put forward a number of concrete practices to this end; including reducing the geographic concentration of arbitral practice in The Hague and expanding the appointment and the training of non-European arbitrators from diverse national backgrounds. The PCA opened an office in Mauritius in 2010, pursuant to the PCA-Mauritius host country agreement, so as to develop arbitral infrastructure and engage the regional arbitration community by participating in educational outreach and training programmes throughout Africa.

3.3.2.2 Accessibility and predictability

As concerning accessibility,[157] international arbitration conducted under the auspices of the PCA presents both certain challenges and potential as relating to costs and party consent to arbitral jurisdiction, as well as some noted advantages, as relating to flexibility of location, language, and procedure. In its origins, the PCA was designed to resolve disputes between states. Through its evolution, the PCA now provides services to various combinations of states, state entities, intergovernmental organizations, and private parties. In principle, the PCA stands to provide a neutral forum for the international adjudication of corporate related human rights abuses without the exhaustion of domestic judicial remedies on the part of the victims. However, non-state actors that access arbitration are typically investors and not other persons or non-commercial actors.[158] Access to international arbitration under the auspices of the PCA would require agreement between the parties, the company and victims, to consent to arbitral jurisdiction ad hoc. International instruments (e.g. direct treaty language in international investment agreements) or specialized PCA rules in the area of business and human rights would need to be adopted so as to facilitate access to international arbitration between companies and victims. Currently, the evidence shows that the mechanism is mostly used by large or extra-large multinational enterprises.[159] This is in part due to the costs related to arbitration.

Prospects for easy access to arbitration administered under the auspices of the PCA and low cost do exist. There are currently methods available to parties for reducing both time and costs, including constituting arbitral tribunals with fewer members; limiting the number of pages of written pleadings; establishing time limits; and limiting the number of days of hearing. In cases relating to corporate related human rights abuses, the arbitration mechanism would have to have regard for the limited resources of victims and enact concrete measures accordingly. Counsel and arbitrator services should be provided pro bono or for a reduced fee. There have been cases where arbitrators and conciliators have been willing to waive all fees.[160] The willingness of international jurists to do pro bono work in cases should not be underestimated. Moreover, the PCA Financial Assistance Fund, which is currently only available for states, could be adapted. This would require a decision by the PCA Member States to change the terms of that fund or to create a new fund with financing that could be open to any party, when the substantive claim relates to human rights.

157 UN Guiding Principles 2011, *supra,* para. 31b. Accessibility is defined as 'being known to all stakeholder groups for whose use they are intended, and providing adequate assistance for those who may face particular barriers to access'.

158 Interview with Lise Johnson, 03 March 2016.

159 D. Behn, 'Legitimacy, Evolution and Growth in Investment Treaty Arbitration: Empirically evaluating the State-of-the-Art', 46(2) *Georgetown Journal of International Law* (2015) 386.

160 Interview with Brooks W. Daly, 24 June 2015.

A great advantage of arbitration conducted under the auspices of the PCA is that it is flexible and procedures can be best adapted to the case at hand, notably in regards to the location of the proceedings, site visits, language(s), and applicable law. While procedural flexibility may detract from predictability[161] of the procedure and the outcome, flexibility can offset barriers traditional to litigation. For instance, in the case where the arbitration is held abroad, there is no need to hire local counsel. As concerning the seat of the arbitration, while the PCA is located in The Hague, arbitration proceedings can be held anywhere in the world the parties agree to. As concerning evidence, for example, evidentiary matters are discretionary to the arbitral tribunal and procedures can be best adapted to the case at hand. There are mass claims procedures explored by working groups at the PCA where lowered standards of proof, burden shifting, and evidentiary sampling were cited as methods to add efficiency and lower cost in special cases.[162] As concerning applicable law, the adoption of a specialized set of arbitral procedural rules in disputes relating to corporate related human rights abuses could include an applicable law clause, or at the least a model applicable law clause, providing for the direct application of international human rights instruments.

3.3.2.3 Transparency and a source of continuous learning

Transparency[163] in international arbitration is fundamental so as to offset concerns surrounding legitimacy of the mechanism and arbitrator accountability. International arbitration in general has been criticized for its confidentiality, but arbitration is not by nature confidential: it follows the agreement of the parties. Parties can agree to have fully transparent proceedings, as evidenced in the *Abyei Arbitration* conducted at the PCA in The Hague between the Government of Sudan and the Sudan People's Liberation Army.[164]

In 2015, the PCA was the first to apply the UNCITRAL Transparency Rules in *Iberdrola, S.A. and Iberdrola Energia. S.A.U. v Bolivia* (PCA Case No. 2015–05). The PCA participated in the negotiation of the UNCITRAL Rules on Transparency in Treaty-based Investor-State Arbitration (2014)

161 UN Guiding Principles 2011, *supra,* para. 31c. Predictability is defined as 'providing a clear and known procedure with an indicative time frame for each stage, and clarity on the types of process and outcome available and means of monitoring implementation.'

162 See generally H. M. Holtzmann and E. Kristjánsdóttir, *International Mass Claims Processes: Legal and Practical Perspectives* (2007) Oxford: Oxford University Press.

163 UN Guiding Principles 2011, *supra,* para. 31e. Transparency is defined as 'keeping parties to a grievance informed about its progress, and providing sufficient information about the mechanism's performance to build confidence in its effectiveness and meet any public interest at stake'.

164 PCA Archives, The Government of Sudan/The Sudan People's Liberation Movement/Army (Abyei Arbitration). Available at http://www.haguejusticeportal.net/Docs/Court%20Documents/PCA/Abyei_Final_Award_EN.pdf, http://legal.un.org/riaa/cases/vol_XXX/145-416.pdf, accessed 11 March 2016.

(UNCITRAL Transparency Rules) and the United Nations Convention on Transparency in Treaty-based Investor-State Arbitration (Mauritius Convention), which was adopted on 10 December 2014 and opened for signature on 17 March 2015, so as to make possible the application of the UNCITRAL Transparency Rules to the existing around 3,000 investment agreements signed before 1 April 2014. The UNICTRAL Transparency Rules and the Mauritius Convention provide the legal basis to open arbitral hearings to the public, to allow interested parties to make submissions to the tribunal, and to make arbitration documents publicly available (the notice of arbitration, the response to the notice of arbitration, the statement of claim, the statement of defence, any further written statements or written submissions by a disputing party, a table listing all exhibits to those documents, if it had been prepared for the proceedings, any written submissions by the non-disputing treaty party/parties and by third parties, transcripts of hearings, where available, and orders, decisions and awards of the arbitral tribunal).[165] As concerning continuous learning,[166] transparency in international arbitration under the auspices of the PCA is essential so that arbitral jurisprudence can be studied and awards can be scrutinized.

3.3.2.4 Rights-compatibility

As concerning rights-compatibility,[167] some of the more prominent arbitration rules in regards to applicable law, including the PCA rules, maintain that arbitral tribunals can apply broad legal standards.[168] Rules of law designated by the parties could provide for the direct application of human rights instruments, although these could run into conflict with mandatory rules in specific jurisdictions that could jeopardize the recognition and enforcement of the eventual award. So as to ensure that outcomes and remedies accord with internationally recognized human rights, a long-term goal of the EU could entail the inclusion of express treaty language providing for the direct application of international human rights instruments into investment agreements.

So as to ensure that outcomes and remedies accord with internationally recognized human rights, the adoption of a specialized set of arbitral procedural rules in disputes relating to corporate related human rights abuses could include oversight of the implementation of the award. This could entail a reporting requirement on award compliance from the parties to the PCA.

165 See UNCITRAL Rules on Transparency in Treaty-based Investor-State Arbitration (2014). Available at: https://www.uncitral.org/pdf/english/texts/arbitration/rules-on-transparency/Rules-on-Transparency-E.pdf, accessed 11 March 2016.

166 UN Guiding Principles 2011, *supra,* para. 31g. A source of continuous learning is defined as 'drawing on relevant measures to identify lessons for improving the mechanism and preventing future grievances and harms.'

167 UN Guiding Principles 2011, *supra,* para. 31f. Rights-compatibility is defined as 'ensuring that outcomes and remedies accord with internationally recognized human rights.'

168 PCA Arbitration Rules 2012, Art. 35; ICSID Convention Article 42(1).

3.3.3 *Concluding remarks*

International arbitration under the auspices of the PCA could be adapted so as to provide uncomplicated access to remedy for victims of corporate related human rights abuses. In its essence, arbitration is a flexible and neutral mechanism for the resolution of cross-border disputes. Currently, the arbitration mechanism under the auspices of the PCA offers certain advantages: notably, the flexibility of procedure in terms of location, language, time limits, evidentiary considerations, as well as the choice, number, and specialization of adjudicators. As the mechanism currently stands, access for victims of corporate related human rights abuses depends on the consent of both the victims and the company. In this regard, it is recommended that the PCA develop specialized arbitration rules for disputes relating to business and human rights, as it has previously done for disputes relating to natural resources and/or the environment and outer space. Such an instrument could formalize and therefore promote some of the aspects important to provide remedy to victims of corporate related human rights abuses; these include financial assistance for costs relating to the arbitration and counsel, transparency, *amicus curiae* participation, collective redress, and oversight of the implementation of the award. Furthermore, the PCA could develop a specialized list of arbitrators and experts in the area of business and human rights, as it has previously done for disputes relating to natural resources and/or the environment and outer space. As relating to costs, the PCA should consider adapting the Financial Assistance Fund so that funds are made available to non-state parties. There are important steps that should be taken that go beyond the PCA, namely, the inclusion by states of express treaty language for the direct application of international human rights instruments and the establishment of arbitral jurisdiction for victims of corporate related human rights abuses in international investment agreements.

3.4 Conclusions and recommendations

Even though many European companies have established some sort of grievance procedures as part of their CSR policies in recent years, the present research shows that fully fledged grievance mechanisms are not yet well developed in Europe. While researchers struggled to even identify company-based grievance mechanisms that preliminarily fulfilled basic quality criteria, detailed research on the two grievance mechanisms revealed that several aspects of the procedures are not yet well-defined, or accessible information is limited. Currently, therefore, both company mechanisms qualify as a set of grievance procedures rather than as fully fledged operational-level grievance mechanisms. The mechanisms are rooted in rather more general corporate social responsibility or compliance standards, emphasizing, for example, anti-corruption policies within companies or community relations. Moreover, some mechanisms have not been widely used to date, making it difficult to evaluate their performance with regard to procedures, outcomes, and efficiency in bringing business-related human rights abuses to the companies' attention.

Both company-based grievance mechanisms use various entry channels for filing complaints, in particular hotlines as well as designated local contact persons (e.g. community liaison officers). In addition, one company-based grievance mechanism also provides the possibility to file more formal written complaints, for instance those addressed to an ombudsman. This makes the grievance mechanisms easily accessible for aggrieved persons and might provide an advantage compared to formal judicial procedures, the requirements of which are often difficult to understand for people without a legal education, and access criteria are challenging to fulfil without legal support. However, the researchers could not establish if persons who might be negatively affected by a company's activity received sufficient information about the grievance mechanisms to allow use of them when needed. Framing the entry channels for filing complaints in the general compliance policy of a company can contribute to a lessened awareness that these channels could also be used in the case of negative human rights impacts. Without the possibility of conducting onsite visits in the framework of this study, it is therefore impossible to say if the necessary information filtered down to each worker or community member, thus effectively ensuring accessibility in practice. Furthermore, it is challenging to assess the extent to which communities and civil society were consulted in the development of the grievance mechanisms, and how they are involved in the implementation of these mechanisms.

Regarding the conduct of grievance procedures, both companies use 'mixed systems', where grievances can be lodged both internally (e.g. through a supervisor or local contact person) and externally (e.g. ombudsperson or external hotline). While internal procedures are arguably even more easily accessible than external procedures, they bear a number of risks, notably a lack of commitment by supervisors to proceed with the complaint and possible reprisals against the complainant. Additionally, such mixed systems might hamper trust of the persons affected in the independence and confidentiality of the process. In fact, concerning the two companies analyzed, further research would be needed in order to assess how confidentiality is ensured in practice if complaints are filed with a company representative such as a supervisor or a contact person for local communities. The same applies to the instruction and training such representatives receive in relation to this matter.

A close connection between the internal and external systems, or even a perceived proximity of the external process to the company, can lead to an increase of distrust even with regard to the external, and thus technically independent, system. An additional risk of applying internal and external systems may be that different stakeholders within the company or related to the company, such as trade unions, workers' councils or compliance officers, are in charge of implementing the different channels, but that there is little exchange among these different stakeholders. While different procedures could potentially also be useful to target different groups of victims, improved exchange would allow a better assessment as to whether the mechanisms established are fully fledged.

In addition, information about the exact responsibilities for each step in the complaints proceedings is limited and, with regard to the cases already dealt with, there is little transparency about the proceedings and outcomes, including clear procedures for providing compensation to those who have been negatively affected. This makes it difficult to predict outcomes and thus persons affected or their counsellors might find it difficult to assess whether they should use one of the company mechanisms or rather try another judicial or non-judicial remedy.

The case studies found that internal grievance mechanisms are mostly used for labour law violations and smaller scale conflicts with local communities. In these cases, some of the procedures can be considered as well-suited for providing relatively quick solutions to less serious human right abuses (e.g. payment for extra hours, obligatory working breaks, unintentional damage to property), ideally without requiring much paperwork on the part of the claimants. However, concerning more complex cases or (potentially) serious violations of human rights, the mechanisms seem too limited. The grievance mechanisms are mostly perceived as tools for labour law violations within the company, its subsidiaries, and – to a certain extent – its suppliers. Only to a limited extent are the mechanisms also seen as mechanisms for addressing negative human rights implications caused by actions of the company.

So far, both companies analyzed in this study are committed to further developing their grievance mechanisms; however, procedures for continuous learning still need to be improved. This concerns both internal review mechanisms and continuous engagement with external stakeholders such as unions or community-based organizations. As, for instance, shown in the case of Siemens, the IFA describes a channel of grievance mechanism that is based on cooperation with the trade union, which is strongly involved in order to increase awareness of the IFA and further institutionalize the lodging of complaints.

Since the proliferation of international arbitration, the default arbitration mechanism has been contemplated by and large for the resolution of cross-border commercial disputes where the primary interests are efficiency and finality. There is evidence that human rights issues have emerged in both commercial and investor-state disputes. Accordingly, if arbitration is to be used in such cases, the mechanism must be adapted as the outcomes inherently impact the public interest, making the correctness of the award and transparency of the proceedings essential. The advantage of international arbitration is that it can provide direct access in a neutral forum for holding companies accountable where national jurisdictions are unavailable or difficult to access. International arbitration is, per se, an external mechanism and if proper procedures are in place, independence towards both parties can be ensured and the outcomes are binding on both parties. However, in contrast to company-based grievance mechanisms, which usually do not involve any direct costs for claimants, international arbitration is costly and a framework to lower the financial burden for victims would be necessary. As concerning international arbitration conducted under the auspices of the PCA, the arbitration mechanism would need to establish procedures that contemplate the particular interests involved in cases where the substantive claims involve human rights; in particular, a set of procedural rules that ensure transparency, review of the award, specialized arbitrators (and their accountability), and financial assistance.

Based on the conclusions, a number of recommendations can be made.

The existence of the Guiding Principles is assessed as an important success factor for non-judicial grievance mechanisms, given that they created awareness.[169] However, the analysis within this research shows that further guidance would be necessary in order to assess for which type of adverse human rights impacts company-based grievance mechanisms are suitable in order to reach a fair remediation. For example, more informal local mechanisms could be useful for monitoring the implementation of agreements, whereas more formalized mechanisms might prove conducive to solutions concerning claims of land rights.[170] It is recommended that further discussion take place within the framework of the UN Working Group on the issue of human rights and transnational corporations and other business enterprises on company-based grievance mechanisms, and for which adverse human rights impacts the most suitable remedies for the persons impacted can be achieved.

Additionally, it is recommended that more information be gathered on the follow up of company-based grievance mechanisms in order to be able to assess whether the mechanism leads to fair remediation. The UN Working Group would need to elaborate in more detail as to which criteria are conducive for an effective, rights-based company-based mechanism, also covering the monitoring of implementation of agreements.

It is recommended that the UN Global Compact's disclosure procedures (Communications on Progress) include further effectiveness criteria and identify in more detail the necessary requirements to be fulfilled concerning operational-level grievance mechanisms in order to ensure that companies implement a fully-fledged operational-level grievance mechanism. At the level of the EU, Member States could also reflect about clear guidance for company-based grievance mechanisms, e.g. in the EU or National Action Plans on Business and Human Rights, taking into account research on best practices and shortcomings.

Regarding the level of the individual company mechanisms, general recommendations are limited as this study has only analyzed two grievance mechanisms

169 Access, *ACCESS to Remedy in Context of Business and Human Rights: Improving the Effectiveness of Non-Judicial Grievance Mechanisms*, (Expert meeting report, 3–4 April 2014), p. 12.

170 In this sense see B. Ganson, *Access to Remedy Through Consensual Processes – Working Paper (ACCESS)* available at http://accessfacility.org/sites/default/files/Working%20Paper%20-%20Access%20to%20remedy%20through%20consensual%20processes.pdf, accessed 3 November 2016, p. 8.

and the conclusions are drawn exclusively on this experience. Bearing this caveat in mind, it is recommended that companies involve civil society – in particular local communities or workers – in the design and implementation of grievance mechanisms. Furthermore, it is advisable to institutionalize exchange on procedures between involved stakeholders, in the case that companies apply a mixed system, involving external and internal channels of lodging complaints. At the same time, confidentiality of individual complaints handled by external stakeholders has to be ensured in order to be able to establish and maintain trust in the procedure.

Entry channels for filing complaints should to a certain extent be separated from the compliance framework in order to strengthen awareness that these mechanisms can also be used for negative human rights impacts. By contrast, independently operated telephone hotlines or online complaints forms, which are available in local languages, can be seen as a positive example of an easy entry point for raising minor issues that can be solved outside courts.

In relation to the Permanent Court of Arbitration, it is recommended that EU Member States give a mandate to the PCA to adopt a set of arbitration rules in disputes relating to corporate related human rights abuses. Such rules should provide for transparency, *amicus curiae* participation, collective redress, specialized arbitrators, financial assistance, and oversight of the implementation of the award.

Furthermore, EU Member States should give a mandate to the PCA to adapt the Financial Assistance Fund to provide financial assistance to non-state parties when the subject matter of the dispute involves corporate related human rights abuses.

Annex: list of interview partners

Case study – Siemens AG

Interview 1: Interview with a representative of 'IG Metall', German Industrial Union of Metal workers on 2 November 2015 per telephone (referred to as 'INT 1, representative of 'IG Metall', 2 November 2015').

Interview 2: Interview with a representative of Siemens AG, Supply Chain Management, on 3 December 2015 per telephone (referred to as 'INT 2, representative of Siemens AG/Supply Chain Management, 3 December 2015').

Interview 3: Interview with a representative of a non-governmental organization, on 2 February 2016 per telephone.

Case study – Statoil

Interview 1: Interview with a representative of Statoil, on 13 January 2016. As the person interviewed objected to it, the information gathered through this interview could not be used for the final case study.

Interview 2: Interview with a representative of a local non-governmental organization, on 7 April 2016, per telephone (referred to as 'INT 2, representative of NGO, 7 April 2016').

Case study – Permanent Court of Arbitration

Interview 1: Interview with Brooks W. Daly, Deputy Secretary-General, Principle Legal Counsellor, Permanent Court of Arbitration, on 24 June 2015.

Interview 2: Interview with Denis Bensaude, Arbitrator (chairperson, sole arbitrator and co-arbitrator) in over fifty cases, under the ICC, LCIA, CCIG, OHADA, CMAP and UNCITRAL rules, as well as in ad hoc arbitrations conducted under the auspices of the Permanent Court of Arbitration, on 3 March 2016.

Interview 3: Interview with Lise Johnson, Head of Investment Law and Policy at the Columbia Center for Sustainable Investment. Previously submitted an *amicus brief* in a case administered by the Permanent Court of Arbitration involving a human rights component; in particular, dealing with the rights of people not party to an investor-state arbitration (in this case, indigenous people), on 3 March 2016.

4 Corporate responsibility to respect human rights vis-à-vis legal duty of care

Cees van Dam and Filip Gregor with contribution from Sandrine Brachotte and Paige Morrow

4.1 Introduction

This chapter deals with the intersection of corporate responsibility to respect human rights and tort law in the context of complex corporate structures and business relationships. More specifically, it considers the relationship between a company's duty of care, on the one hand, and the same company's responsibility to seek to prevent or mitigate adverse human rights impacts linked to its operations, products or services by its business relationships, such as those concerning subsidiary companies (as a headquarters, parent, or controlling company), contractors, and other business partners. In this regard, this chapter proposes three types of legal reform: a disclosure obligation for a company as regards the control it exercises over its business partners (Scenario I), a rebuttable presumption of control a company exercises over its business partners (Scenario II), and a statutory duty for a company to conduct human rights due diligence (Scenario III).[1]

The analysis builds on the answers to two consecutive surveys solicited from distinguished legal experts from France, Germany, the Netherlands, Sweden, Switzerland, and the UK. Altogether, the authors received twenty opinions from

1 This chapter was written by Cees van Dam, Professor of International Business and Human Rights at the Rotterdam School of Management (Erasmus University), and Visiting Professor at King's College London, and Filip Gregor, Head of Responsible Companies Section at Frank Bold, a purpose driven law firm, with the contribution from Sandrine Brachotte, Legal Consultant at Frank Bold, and Paige Morrow, Head of Brussels Operations at Frank Bold. The authors would like to thank the following individuals who provided inputs through the consultation: Daniel Augenstein (Germany), Anne Scheltema Beduin (Netherlands), Stéphane Brabant (France), David Chivers, QC (UK), Sandra Cossart (France), Liesbeth Enneking (Netherlands), Ingrid Gubbay (UK), Patrick Harty (UK), Nicola Jägers (Netherlands), Rasmus Kløcker Larse (Sweden), Yvon Martinet (France), Robert McCorquodale (UK), Sarah McGrath (United States), Krishnendu Mukherjee (UK), Lucas Roorda (Netherlands), Urs Rybi (Switzerland), Channa Samkalden (Netherlands), John Sherman (US), Christopher Schuller (Germany), Gwynne Skinne (US).

experts, whose names are listed in the acknowledgements. The aim of these surveys and of this work was threefold:

1. Clarify obstacles connected to tort law that undermine the realization of corporate responsibility to respect human rights.
2. Identify the most feasible and effective reforms to overcome these obstacles and improve access to remedy for victims of human rights abuse.
3. Consider the scope and other characteristics of such reforms, taking into account the principles of tort law, precedents, and legitimate interests of corporate actors.

The authors have examined eight different scenarios for reforms and a number of associated questions, including role and definition of control in the context of corporate groups and business relationships, connection between the definition of human rights violations and the tort concept of harm, the effect of corporate statutory duties on the position of victims, and the causation between meeting or failing standards of care and harm suffered. Three of these reform scenarios are presented alongside assessment of several options concerning their scope.

These scenarios consider the situation of a legal action launched before the court of an EU member state by victims of corporate human rights abuses against an EU company that holds control over another company that has caused or contributed to the abuse in a non-EU state. The legal basis of such action in tort law is that the defendant-company breached its duty of care by causing, contributing or not preventing a human rights abuse in the operations of another company or other entity over which it exercised control with respect to the harmful activities.

This does not consider the cases where the liability of the parent company is based on piercing the corporate veil, under corporate law. The conditions for piercing the corporate veil differ in different countries, but in general they include situations where the subsidiary had no free will, was set up for fraudulent purposes, or established to avoid an existing obligation.

This chapter proposes three options for legal reform, which would also be complementary to one another if all are adopted:

- Scenario I: facilitating victims' access to evidence of the defendant-company's control over its business partner, e.g. subsidiary or contractor that has committed the alleged human rights violation.
- Scenario II: in terms of burden of proof, presuming the existence of such control when certain conditions are met that show control prima facie.
- Scenario III: introducing a company's statutory duty to identify, prevent, and take action to cease human rights abuses by its business partners, analogous to the human rights due diligence outlined in the UN Guiding Principles.

Before discussing each of these scenarios in detail in separate sections, this chapter briefly sets out their legal context.

4.2 Legal context

4.2.1 Implementing the UN Guiding Principles

The EU law on jurisdiction in civil matters[2] allows victims of corporate human rights abuse to bring a tort claim against a company domiciled in the EU, including when the harm that provides basis for the claim occurred outside of the EU. Often, this is the only option for victims of corporate human rights abuses committed in non-EU states to get access to remedy, due to the corruption or lack of capacity of judiciary in their countries, or because the company responsible for the harm has limited assets located in these countries.

The UN Guiding Principle 26 outlines the duty of a state to ensure the effectiveness of their judicial mechanisms and remove barriers that could lead to a denial of access to remedy.[3] The commentary to this principle states: 'Legal barriers that can prevent legitimate cases involving business-related human rights abuse from being addressed can arise where, for example: The way in which legal responsibility is attributed among members of a corporate group under domestic criminal and civil laws facilitates the avoidance of appropriate accountability; [or] Where claimants face a denial of justice in a host State [where the harmful event has occurred] and cannot access home State courts [where the company-defendant is domiciled] regardless of the merits of the claim.'[4]

The possibility for victims of human rights abuses to start civil proceedings against the company that is controlling, or greatly influencing, the company which has caused the harm is in line with the scope of the corporate responsibility to respect human rights, and the human rights due diligence process relating thereto, described in the UN Guiding Principles. This twin concept consists of two elements that require business enterprises to:

(a) avoid causing or contributing to adverse human rights impacts through their own activities, and address such impacts when they occur;
(b) seek to prevent or mitigate adverse human rights impacts that are directly linked to their operations, products or services by their business relationships, even if they have not contributed to those impacts.

These elements bear similarity to the duty of care concept in tort law, which requires a person that is found liable of having acted with negligence thereby

2 EU Regulation No. 1215/2012 of 12 December 2012 on jurisdiction and the recognition and enforcement of judgments in civil and commercial matters (recast), *OJ L 351/1*, 20 December 2012, Art. 2.

3 Guiding Principle 26 states as follows: 'States should take appropriate steps to ensure the effectiveness of domestic judicial mechanisms when addressing business-related human rights abuses, including considering ways to reduce legal, practical and other relevant barriers that could lead to a denial of access to remedy.'

4 UN Doc. A/HRC/17/31, 21 March 2011, Commentary on Guiding Principle 26.

causing harm to another, to compensate the victim of such harm.[5] A breach of the corporate responsibility to respect human rights can, therefore, amount to a breach of the duty of care.

The question of under which conditions a company can be held liable for acts of other legally separate persons such as subsidiaries,[6] contractors, and other business partners violating human rights, has only rarely been subject of court decisions in the Member States of the EU.[7] Therefore, the answer to this question is subject to debate. One of the obstacles for victims is to prove that the company exercised control over the relevant activities of the (legal) person(s) causing the harmful situation, which depends on the circumstances of the case. If the company exercises control it is usually only liable if it can be considered to have breached the duty of care towards the third parties suffering harm as a result of the situation. Although the exact requirements will differ across jurisdictions, a pivotal consideration for this breach of the duty will be whether, considering the likeliness and magnitude of the potential harm suffered by the victims of a human rights violation, the company should have taken measures to prevent the harm from occurring or to mitigate its consequences.

In practice, one of the major problems for victims to access remedy is that they are usually not in a position to prove the existence of such control. Indeed, in many situations the victims lack evidence to prove their case, because much of the relevant information on the control relationship in corporate structures and other relationships is not within their reach.

4.2.2 Following the general legal trend

The three scenarios that are outlined in this chapter correspond with the general tendency in law to improve transparency and accountability in the operations of business enterprises. In Europe, there have been several attempts to embed the corporate duty to prevent human rights impacts by business partners (i.e. by their subsidiaries and contractors), both in company law and civil law. First, in 2014 the EU adopted the non-financial reporting directive, which will require large corporations to report on how they address risks of human rights impacts linked to their operations, including by products, services, and business

5 For further details, see A. Sanders, 'The impact of the 'Ruggie framework' and the United Nations guiding principles on business and human rights on transnational human rights litigation'. In *The business and human rights landscape: moving forward, looking back,* K. E. Bravo & J. Martin (eds.) (2015) Cambridge University Press: Cambridge, 288–315.

6 In this chapter the term 'subsidiary' includes all legal entities that are part of the group, including subsubsidiaries.

7 See, for example, the English cases of *Chandler v Cape* [2012] EWCA Civ 525 and *Thompson v The Renwick Group plc* (2014) EWCA Civ 635.

relationships.[8] The EU institutions discuss further steps in the area of conflict minerals[9] and garment supply chains.[10]

Second, in the UK, the Modern Slavery Act (2015) requires businesses to publish an annual statement that confirms the steps taken to ensure that slavery and human trafficking are not taking place in the business (or in any supply chain).[11]

Third, the French Parliament is discussing a reform of the Commercial Code recognizing a duty of vigilance of parent companies with content and scope analogous to the concepts outlined in the UN Guiding Principles.[12]

Fourth, in Switzerland a coalition of 77 organizations launched a popular initiative that aims to put to a public vote in referendum a proposal for legal reform that would oblige companies to carry out due diligence and introduce their liability for human rights abuses and environmental violations caused abroad by companies under their control.[13]

In March 2016, the Committee of Ministers of the Council of Europe adopted a recommendation[14] providing that Member States should take measures that: (a) encourage or, where appropriate, require, that business enterprises carry our human rights due diligence throughout their operations; (b) encourage and, where appropriate, require such businesses to provide information on their efforts

8 EU Directive 2014/95/EU of 22 October 2014 amending Directive 2013/34/EU as regards disclosure of non-financial and diversity information by certain large undertakings and groups, *OJ L 330/1*, 15 November 2014.

9 See C. Barbière, EU institutions still divided over conflict minerals (5 February 2016). Retrieved from EurActive website: http://www.euractiv.com/section/development-policy/news/eu-institutions-still-divided-over-conflict-minerals/, accessed 30 May 2016.

10 On 25 April 2016, the European Commission hosted the first High-level Conference on responsible supply chain management in the garment sector, to promote successful existing initiatives, including from Member States and industry, and provide a platform for continuing the dialogue at EU level (see European Commission, High-level Conference on Responsible Management of the Supply Chain in the Garment Sector (n.d.). Retrieved from https://ec.europa.eu/europeaid/news-and-events/high-level-conference-responsible-management-supply-chain-garment-sector_en, accessed 30 May 2016).

11 *Modern Slavery Act 2015* (cl. 30).

12 See additional and up-to-date information on the official French website of legal information: http://www.vie-publique.fr/actualite/panorama/texte-discussion/proposition-loi-relative-au-devoir-vigilance-societes-meres-entreprises-donneuses-ordre.html, accessed 30 May 2016. The latest draft of the bill, as approved by the French National Assembly on 23 March 2016 is available at: http://www.assemblee-nationale.fr/14/ta/ta0708.asp, accessed 30 May 2016.

13 See E. Umlas, Human rights due diligence: Swiss civil society pushes the envelope (n.d.). Retrieved from the Business and Human Rights Resource Centre, http://business-humanrights.org/en/human-rights-due-diligence-swiss-civil-society-pushes-the-envelope, accessed 30 May 2016; see also the official website: http://www.konzern-initiative.ch/ accessed 30 May 2016.

14 Council of Europe (Committee of Ministers), Recommendation CM/Rec(2016)3 on human rights and business, 2 March 2016.

on corporate responsibility to respect human rights;[15] and (c) ensure that human rights abuses caused by business enterprises give rise to civil liability, and examine the possibility of creating civil causes of action against business enterprises that cause human rights abuses as a consequence of a failure to carry out adequate due diligence processes to prevent or mitigate risks to human rights.[16]

In November 2014, the Office of the UN High Commissioner for Human Rights launched an initiative 'to make domestic legal responses fairer and more effective for victims of business-related human rights abuses, particularly in the most severe cases.' The initiative, called the 'Accountability and Remedy Project' (ARP), 'aims to deliver credible and concrete recommendations and guidance to States to enable more effective implementation of the Access to Remedy pillar of the UN Guiding Principles.' On 10 May 2016, the High Commissioner published the ARP final report, which will be discussed at the 32nd session of the UN Human Rights Council in June 2016.[17] This report includes guidance to UN Member States that 'The principles for assessing corporate liability under domestic private law regimes are properly aligned with the responsibility of companies to exercise human rights due diligence across their operations.'[18]

Finally, there are multiple examples in law recognizing the liability of companies for the acts of other entities, such as their subsidiaries, business partners, or agents. These examples can be found in environmental law,[19] labour law,[20] and criminal law.[21] The conditions for liability differ depending on the nature

15 *Ibid.*, paras 20 and 21.

16 *Ibid.*, para. 32 and Explanatory Memoradum, para. 54.

17 UN Doc. A/HRC/32/19, 10 May 2016.

18 *Ibid.*, Policy Objective no. 14.

19 See, for example, U.S. Comprehensive Environmental Response, Compensation, and Liability Act – 'CERCLA' (42 U.S.C. § 9601–9675) and Canadian Waste Management Act, R.S.B.C. 1996, c. 482. In *United States v Bestfoods*, No. 97–454 (1998) the Supreme Court of the United States held that parent companies can be directly liable under CERCLA § 107(a) if they are directly involved in the subsidiary's management of hazardous substances.

20 The Directive 2009/52/EC of the European Parliament and of the Council of 18 June 2009 providing for minimum standards on sanctions and measures against employers of illegally staying third-country nationals (*OJ L 168,* 30 June 2009) provides that both an employer who employed illegally staying third-country nationals and a contractor to whom the employer was subcontractor, should be liable for financial sanctions and back payments. In the UK, the Pensions Act 2004 (cl. 35) provides that, if the pension fund established by the service company that employs employees of the group of companies goes into deficit, the other group companies cannot insulate themselves from that deficit and can be made to contribute to the fund to meet the liabilities to the employees.

21 In the UK, s. 7 of the Bribery Act 2010 (cl. 23), recognizes a criminal offence of the failure of commercial organizations to prevent bribery on their behalf. Bribery may be carried out by an employee, an agent, a subsidiary, or another third party, as found in s. 8. In France, on 25 September 2012, the Cour de cassation in Paris found the company Total liable for a criminal offence as regards the tanker Erika oil spill in 1999. Erika was operated by a subcontractor of Total's subsidiary. The court has made clear that criminal liability could be found liable beyond legal separation made between two companies when de facto they work as a single one, so that such separation can be considered as a 'legal fiction'. (Cass (crim.), judgement no. 3439, 25 September 2015).

and the purpose of the regulation. In some instances, the liability of the company is absolute, such as, for example, in competition law. In other cases, liability is built on principles similar to the human rights due diligence concept, that is, that the company may discharge its liability if it took all reasonable steps to prevent the violation.

4.3 Scenarios

4.3.1 Scenario I: access to evidence on control

4.3.1.1 Background

The exact conditions under which a company is liable for not having prevented a human rights violation by its business partner (e.g. a subsidiary or a contractor) have not yet been fleshed out comprehensively in the case law and they are subject to debate. Generally speaking, however, liability of the company will require the victim to prove that the company breached a duty of care that it owed to him, and that his damage was caused by this breach. One of the conditions for the breach of a company's duty of care, when this company did not cause the harm itself, is that the company exercised sufficient control over the business partner causing the harm, and that the company did not use this control in such a way as to prevent the business partner from violating human rights, while if 'acting like a reasonably acting company put in the same conditions',[22] the company would have done so. A pivotal consideration for this will be whether, considering the likeliness and magnitude of the potential harm to third parties by violating human rights, the company should have taken measures to prevent the harm from occurring or to mitigate its consequences.

Control can be of a formal character (such as in parent-subsidiaries relationships) or mainly factual (such as in supply chain situations). It may also imply that the company one way or another had the power to influence the conduct of its business partner. The case law does not yet provide a clear definition as to what amounts to sufficient control. The courts have to assess this on a case-by-case basis and the assessment may differ per jurisdiction. The usual default position is that it is for the victim to provide the court with satisfactory evidence that the company exercised sufficient control over its business partner to influence its conduct. This illustrates the importance of victims gaining access to the relevant information.

Although much evidence of a company's business relationships may be collected and obtained by claimants from publicly available sources, this is usually

22 The 'reasonable company' is defined based on several criteria that depend, notably, on the size and sector of the company.

a very time-consuming and costly affair. Moreover, claimants can simply not access evidence that is in the realm of the company. The latter is particularly problematic with respect to evidence that a company controlled or influenced the actions which caused or contributed to the harm, but which were carried out by a third party, such as a company's subsidiary or a contractor.

One of the main reasons why victims of human rights abuses often cannot get access to relevant information to demonstrate the liability of a company is that the national rules on disclosure of evidence that are in force in the forum country often do not allow for this.

In this respect, common law and civil law systems differ considerably. Roughly speaking, common law systems of civil procedure contain general rules on disclosure of evidence[23] whereas civil law systems of civil procedure do not.[24] In England and Wales, there is a general duty to disclose evidence relevant to the case under the Civil Procedure Rules (CPR). In practice, this means that before the trial 'a party discloses a document by stating that the document exists or has existed' and 'a party to whom a document has been disclosed has a right to inspect that document' and obtain a copy. 'Document' has a very broad meaning and includes anything in which information of any description is recorded, covering any form of electronic document, on any media device. The only limitations are the overriding principle of proportionality of the disclosure requests, which should be limited by either date, persons, place or categories, and the fact that privileged documents are limited to inspection only.

In civil law systems, of civil procedure this option is not available. It is usually for the claimant to request the court to order the defendant to disclose specific documents. The burden of adequately specifying the documents and to justify a legitimate interest in inspection of those documents is on the claimant. The courts are generally very reluctant to allow such a request and to order the defendant to disclose one or more of the specified documents.[25] This means that companies have no incentive to be transparent about their involvement

23 In this chapter the English term 'disclosure' will be used. In the US this phenomenon is known as 'discovery'. The rules differ in detail but not in principle.

24 In some jurisdictions like the Netherlands, the courts may require a defendant to provide information enabling the claimant to substantiate his claim. See Hoge Raad 20 November 1987, *Nederlandse Jurisprudentie* 1988/500 (Timmer/Deutman) and Hoge Raad 18 February 1994, *Nederlandse Jurisprudentie* 1994/368 (Schepers/De Bruijn). So far, such a rule has, however, not been applied in cases against parent companies with respect to their control over subsidiaries. In the Netherlands, legislative reform with respect to disclosure is also considered, but no specific action has yet been taken.

25 An example of a small breakthrough is Court of Appeal The Hague, *Milieudefensie a.o./ Shell*, 18 December 2015. See Liesbeth F. H. Enneking, 'Multinationals and Transparency in Foreign Direct Liability Cases. The Prospects for Obtaining Evidence under the Dutch Civil Procedural Regime on the Production of Exhibits,' 3 *Dovenschmidt Quarterly* (2013) 134–147.

because this might give a clue to claimants as to which documents they would like to request. For the claimants, this is an unfortunate position as it involves the risk of requesting the wrong documents or not all the relevant documents.

4.3.1.2 Description of Scenario I

Civil law jurisdictions introduce a specific disclosure obligation in a civil court procedure with respect to the control a parent company exercises over its subsidiaries and contractors. This would oblige a company-defendant to disclose all details of the control it exercises over its subsidiaries and contractors, and its general involvement in the management of its subsidiaries and contractors as well as its control and involvement in the specific case connected to the claim, inasmuch as this information is relevant for assessing the company-defendant's duty of care. The aim of this scenario is to limit the current discretion of the courts and to extend the basis for claimants to access information, albeit on a limited aspect of the liability question as a whole.

Effective disclosure is also key to brokering any possible early dispute resolution where appropriate (as often happens in common law jurisdictions by pre-trial out of court settlements). Thus it contributes to the limitation of time and costs of the proceedings.

This reform does not concern common law jurisdictions because they already provide for extensive pre-trial disclosure obligations.

4.3.1.3 Feasibility

For the scenario to be feasible a number of issues need to be addressed, particularly with respect to the question as to which information is legally required.

In this regard, the concept of control needs to be clarified and developed. Defining such control could be done in legislation. The legislation could provide guidelines with respect to control and leave it to the court that hears the case to apply these guidelines, specify the disclosure obligation, and tailor it to the circumstances of the case. This would allow the court to keep the disclosure obligation up to date. In fact, circumstances under which a parent company may be held liable might change over time and so may the information on control that is relevant to assess the duty of care.

The issues regarding confidentiality and competitiveness can be dealt with in line with provisions in common law jurisdictions that contain strong safeguards in this respect.

This scenario may be implemented as a procedural rule or as a substantive rule. Implementing it as a procedural rule would imply amending the national codes of procedure, which might be challenging for Member States of the EU. Implementing it as a substantive rule would mean that according to the Rome II

Regulation on applicable law,[26] the court must in principle apply the law of the place where the harm occurred. There are several exceptions provided in the Regulation, but it is disputed whether they would fit this scenario.[27] This issue needs to be clarified by drafting the reform as an overriding mandatory provision in the sense of Article 16, which would allow the court to apply it as a mandatory provision of the law of the forum country, which will usually be the country where the parent company is based, instead of the law of the country where the harm occurred.

4.3.1.4 Effectiveness

In order for the information made available to be effective, the document subject to disclosure in court should not be limited to general and formal documents but should include emails and reports of meetings, etc. Again, this can be brought in line with existing disclosure obligations in common law jurisdictions like England.

4.3.2 Scenario II: rebuttable presumption of control

4.3.2.1 Background

The background for Scenario II is the same as in Scenario I. That is, in current tort law, the victim-claimant has the burden of proof with respect to the control exercised by the company-defendant over its subsidiary, or another business partner, which caused the harm. The problem as regards access to remedy is the lack of information for claimants in this respect.

4.3.2.2 Description of Scenario II

This scenario requires a court to accept prima facie evidence[28] that a company exercises control over its subsidiaries or other business partners, and then shifts the burden of proof to the company to prove that it did not exercise such control (the shift only concerns control, not the duty of care and the breach of duty). The court could use prima facie control definitions from, for example, accounting law, thus assuming control: (i) if the company controls the majority

26 EU Regulation No. 864/2007 of 11 July 2007 on the law applicable to non-contractual obligations (Rome II), *OJ L-199/40*.

27 A provision of domestic provision can be applied instead of a provision of the normally applicable law if the latter provision is manifestly incompatible with the public policy (*ordre public*) of the forum (Art. 26). Domestic mandatory provisions shall always be applied in addition the normally applicable law (Art. 16).

28 Prima facie evidence means evidence that upon initial examination appears to support a case.

of shareholders' voting rights; (ii) if the company has appointed or has the right to appoint the majority of the subsidiary's management; or (iii) if the company has the power to exercise or exercises dominant influence on its subsidiary.[29] If the company would not meet such a threshold, the court would not accept the existence of control prima facie, so the victims would have to demonstrate the existence of such control under ordinary principles of law (i.e. as usual).

This scenario is limited to claims concerning the control a company exercises as regards its potential duty of care in tort. It does not apply to other types of disputes, such as breach of contract.

The disclosure obligation described in Scenario I allows the claimant to obtain information in order to prove that the parent exercised control over the subsidiary or another business partner in the specific case, while this Scenario II goes a small step further by, under certain conditions, assuming a rebuttable presumption of control. In both scenarios the requirements for liability (duty of care, the breach of that duty, causation and damage) will still need to be established. However, both scenarios will be of considerable help for claimants in having access to remedy for the abuse of their human rights.

4.3.2.3 Feasibility

The scenario, if implemented as a reform of substantive law, would not be applied in cases for which it would be designed. The reason for this is that, according to the Rome II Regulation on applicable law,[30] the court must in principle apply the law of the place where the harm occurred. There are several exceptions provided in the Regulation, but it is disputed whether they would fit this scenario.[31] This issue needs to be clarified by drafting the reform as an overriding mandatory provision in the sense of Article 16, which would allow the court to apply it as a mandatory provision of the law of the forum country, which will usually be the country where the parent company is based, instead of the law of the country where the harm occurred.

The scenario represents a gradual rather than a departure in principle from existing law. Courts may already be able to partially alleviate the burden of proof placed on claimants where the facts speak for themselves (known as '*res ipsa loquitur*'). They should be encouraged to do so also for the questions of

29 In accounting law meeting these criteria means that the accounts of this company need to be included in the accounts of the group (See Directive 2013/34/EU of 26 June 2013 on the annual financial statements, consolidated financial statements and related reports of certain types of undertakings, *OJ L 182*, 29 June 2013, pp. 19–76).

30 EU Regulation No 864/2007 of 11 July 2007 on the law applicable to non-contractual obligations (Rome II), *OJ L-199/40.*

31 A provision of domestic provision can be applied instead of a provision of the normally applicable law if the latter provision is manifestly incompatible with the public policy (*ordre public*) of the forum (Art. 26). Domestic mandatory provisions shall always be applied in addition the normally applicable law (Art. 16).

a parent company's control of its business partners, although the full implementation of this scenario requires a statutory reform.

The rebuttable presumption is a less radical approach than the option of a full reversal of the burden of proof of control, because it still requires claimants to present prima facie evidence. It does not radically change the legal situation of the defendant companies, in that it would not result in automatic liability for the conduct of their subsidiaries, or cause any obviously onerous issues with respect to competitiveness and confidentiality.

4.3.2.4 Effectiveness

Just like Scenario I, Scenario II requires a clear definition of the concept of the control, which should be flexible so that the courts can adapt its specific contents to the evolution of business behaviour and practices.

The proposal can be effective in helping claimants to address a failure of a company to adequately supervise its subsidiaries. However, it does not address other evidential gaps, for example regarding difficulties with respect to the scientific, technical and legal connection between the victims' injuries and company's conduct, which would need to be addressed by a more far-reaching reform of evidence disclosure.

4.3.3 Scenario III: statutory duty for a company to conduct human rights due diligence

4.3.3.1 Background

In most legal systems, it is difficult for victims of corporate human rights abuses to establish that a company owed them a duty of care not only to prevent its subsidiaries,[32] but also its suppliers and other business partners, from committing human rights abuses against them and/or to mitigate the consequences of any such abuses that have already occurred. There is very little case law clarifying this point and, if it does, such duties are only accepted, if at all, under strict and narrow conditions.

4.3.3.2 Description of Scenario III

This scenario proposes making human rights due diligence (HRDD) compulsory by creating statutory duties to identify, prevent, mitigate and cease human rights abuses for which the company conducting the HRDD is directly or indirectly responsible, that is, those caused by its business partners, over which the company can exercise control, and by providing remedies (damages, injunctions) in

32 See with respect to parents and subsidiaries, the English cases of *Chandler v Cape* [2012] EWCA Civ 525 and *Thompson v The Renwick Group plc* (2014) EWCA Civ 635.

the case that one or more of these duties should be breached. The HRDD of the UN Guiding Principles still goes considerably further than this scenario, as it is not limited to situations of legal or factual control.

The statutory duty to conduct HRDD implies a duty of care owed by the company to victims of human rights abuse that corresponds with the extent of the HRDD. Liability of the company would depend on the question of whether it effectively carried out the HRDD, and whether there was a sufficient causal connection between the harm suffered by the victims and the lack of HRDD by the company.

Conducting HRDD is not an absolute standard but depends on the circumstances of the case.[33] In this respect, the statutory standard will be comparable with the general tort law standard of 'acting as a reasonable person'. It would mean that if the company did not meet the HRDD requirements, it can be considered not to have acted as a 'reasonable person' or a 'reasonable company' put in the same conditions and would therefore be liable subject to certain additional conditions.[34] This 'reasonable company' is based on several criteria, such as the magnitude of the risk of a human rights violation, the burden for the company (in terms of time and costs) to take precautionary measures, as well as the size and sector of the company. Generally accepted industry standards would further inform the assessment of the reasonableness of an action taken to discharge the duty.

If the company has breached its duty by not properly carrying out HRDD, it will be liable for the damage that occurred as a consequence of this breach. This will, for example, be the case if carrying out HRDD would have enabled the company to identify the human rights risk that threatened the victim and to take measures to prevent the human rights violation or to limit the consequences of such violation.

If these requirements are met, the company is obliged to pay compensation for the damage suffered by the claimants.

This statutory duty may not only be enforced by victims of human rights abuses in the framework of tort law but at the same time also by public law measures. As regards the latter, one may think of enforcement by a public body (regulator) that is entitled to fine a company that breaches such duties or order the company to refrain from certain conduct or to do something, for example, providing an effective remedy for a human rights violation in which the company was involved.[35] This way of public enforcement could be akin to rules applying in competition law, consumer protection law, and financial services law.

33 Compare UN Guiding Principle 17B: 'Human rights due diligence [. . .] will vary in complexity with the size of the business enterprise, the risk of severe human rights impacts, and the nature and context of its operations'.

34 See section entitled 'Description of Scenario III – comparison with existing tort law'.

35 For example, in the UK, regulators have the statutory power to order a company to pay compensation to individuals or companies that have been negatively affected by the breach of statutory regulatory duties with respect to market behaviour (See Financial Services and Markets Act 2000 (cl. 8), s. 212).

DESCRIPTION OF SCENARIO III – VARIATIONS

Some variations of this scenario are conceivable. First, the company's liability might initially be limited to subsidiaries over which it exercises control, for example, as provided for in the definition in accounting law as suggested in Scenario II. Later, the scope can be extended to other business partners over whom the company exercises sufficient control (such as companies in the supply chain, for example, direct contractors that are not also the company's subsidiaries). For these latter cases, it needs to be established how much control is needed to create a legal duty and, in conjunction with this, what such a duty would entail. The content of this duty can be partially clarified by the emerging standards for value chain responsibility, such as the OECD general[36] and sector-wise due diligence standards,[37] and government supported multi-stakeholder initiatives such as the Dutch Garment Covenant.[38]

Second, the company's liability might initially be limited to certain specific human rights risks. This may link to certain human rights or to a certain level of breach such as 'serious human rights abuses'. Alternatively, it may link to internationally recognized standards, for example, with respect to environmental harm. Limiting the scope of the statutory duty in this way would also help to provide a private right of action in common law jurisdictions.[39]

Third, the burden of proof with respect to the breach of this statutory duty is, in principle, on the claimant. This burden may be alleviated with respect to information that is in the realm of the company in line with Scenario I and with respect to the legal control in line with Scenario II. It is, however, also conceivable to reverse the burden of proof of the breach of the duty altogether, or for the causation between the failure to conduct HRDD and the damage. This would mean that it is for the company to prove that it carried out due diligence/acted as would a reasonable company. Such a scenario would strengthen the position of victims of human rights abuses even further than by

36 See OECD Guidelines for Multinational Enterprises available at: http://www.oecd.org/corporate/mne, accessed 30 May 2016. As of May 2016, OECD develops detailed due diligence guidance for responsible business conduct.

37 See, for example, OECD Due Diligence Guidance for Responsible Supply Chains of Minerals from Conflict-Affected and High-Risk Areas available at: http://www.oecd.org/corporate/mne/mining.htm, accessed 30 May 2016; OECD-FAO Guidance for Responsible Agricultural Supply Chains available at: http://www.oecd.org/daf/inv/investment-policy/rbc-agriculture-supply-chains.htm, accessed 30 May 2016; and the Draft OECD Due Diligence Guidance for Responsible Supply Chains in the Garment and Footwear Sector available at: https://mneguidelines.oecd.org/Draft-for-Consultation-Due-Diligence-Guidance-Responsible-Supply-Chains-Garment-Footwear-Sector.pdf, accessed 30 May 2016.

38 The full document is available in Dutch on the webpage: http://www.ser.nl/~/media/files/internet/publicaties/overige/2010_2019/2016/convenant-duurzame-kleding-textiel.ashx, accessed 30 May 2016. The English translation is available at: http://eu-roadmap.nl/wp-content/uploads/2016/05/agreement-sustainable-garment-textile.pdf, accessed 30 May 2016.

39 See section entitled: 'Description of Scenario III – Comparison with existing tort law'.

introducing a statutory HRDD duty and it would lower their threshold for access to justice. Still, in such a variation, the victim would need to prove the basic facts, such as that he suffered harm because of a human rights violation by a subordinate company. It may then be up to the company–defendant to prove that it did not breach its duty, for example, because it did not have sufficient control over the violating company, or because it could not reasonably prevent the violation from happening.

Fourth, the legal duty could initially be limited to large companies.

DESCRIPTION OF SCENARIO III – RELATIONSHIP WITH UN GUIDING PRINCIPLES

The proposal brings the company's duty of care to business relationships in line with the scope of the HRDD in the UN Guiding Principles, which require companies to address risks of human rights abuses which may be directly linked to its operations, products, and services by its business relationships alongside those that the company may cause or contribute to. However, Scenario III is limited to situations of legal and factual control, whereas the HRDD of the UN Guiding Principles is not.

The traditional focus of due diligence is on identifying risks. This is understandable from the perspective of the traditional aim of carrying out due diligence: to identify (hidden) risks in the books of a company that is about to be taken over or becomes part of a merger. However, HRDD has a broader focus. It is not only aimed at identifying human rights risks but also at *preventing* and *mitigating* them. This implicitly includes *ceasing* the risk from continuing to exist. If a human rights violation occurs, the question is therefore whether the company's HRDD could and should have avoided it, ceased it, or limited its consequences.

DESCRIPTION OF SCENARIO III – COMPARISON WITH EXISTING TORT LAW

This scenario would establish a statutory duty for a company to carry out HRDD. Apart from this new step, the conditions under which the company would be liable are the same as under traditional tort law.

First, the statutory duty must have been breached, which means that it has to be established that the company did not effectively carry out HRDD.

Second, it needs to be established that the claimants have suffered damage and that this damage was caused or contributed to by the company's breach of duty of carrying out HRDD. The burden of proof for the breach of the duty, causation and damage remains, in principle, on the claimants. Claimants may, therefore, still need help from Scenarios I and II, which partially alleviate this burden with respect to the question of control.

Third, under English law, the new statute must either include an express provision for civil liability or it must be clear from the context of the statute that it allows a person damaged by the breach to bring an action for breach of statutory duty. In fact, in common law, a breach of statutory duty does not, by itself, give rise to any private law cause of action.[40] For example, the statutory duties owed by company directors to the company exist for the benefit of its members, and not for the benefit of third parties.[41] As a result, a person suffering a human rights abuse because of a breach of a statutory duty will not necessarily be eligible to launch a legal action for damages. Conversely, in civil law jurisdictions, the breach of a statutory duty does, in principle, give someone who suffers damage because of this breach a right to compensation against the company. However, the scope of this statutory duty may imply that it does not protect certain victims, or not against certain types of harm. This may follow from the context in which the statute was adopted by parliament or from the wording of the statutory duty.

DESCRIPTION OF SCENARIO III – COMPARISON WITH EXISTING LEGAL PROPOSALS

i) The Swiss responsible business initiative In Switzerland a coalition of seventy-seven organizations launched the Swiss Responsible Business Initiative (RBI), which is a popular initiative that aims to put to a public vote in referendum a proposal for legal reform that would oblige companies to carry out due diligence and introduce their liability for human rights abuses and environmental violations caused abroad by companies under their control.[42] A popular initiative succeeds if the initiators manage to collect 100,000 signatures from Swiss citizens across eighteen months. As of April 2016, twelve months after the launch of the initiative, the initiative collected 140,000 signatures. Just before the launch of the initiative, the Swiss parliament first accepted but then narrowly voted down a motion calling for mandatory HRDD.[43]

RBI aims to embed the key principles of the corporate responsibility to respect human rights as outlined in the UN Guiding Principles into Swiss law. To this end, it presents a constitutional proposal that has four elements:

- Duty to respect: companies have to respect internationally recognized human rights and international environmental standards, and must ensure that these

40 See M. A. Jones *et al.* (eds.) *Clerk & Lindsell on Torts* (2014) London: Sweet & Maxwell, 9–06.
41 Companies Act 2006 (cl. 46), s. 172.
42 English translation of the initiative is available on the official website: http://konzern-initiative.ch/wp-content/uploads/2015/11/150421_sccj_factsheet_5_-_responsible_business_initiative.pdf, accessed 30 May 2016.
43 See further information in the complication from OECD Insights Blog prepared for OECD Week 2015: *How international investment is shaping the global economy*, OECD 2015, 8, available at: http://www.oecd.org/investment/2015-international-investment-blog-compilation.pdf, accessed 30 May 2016.

standards are respected also by companies under their control. Control is to be determined according to the factual circumstances and may also result through the exercise of power in a business relationship.

- Mandatory due diligence: companies are required to carry out due diligence. In line with the UN Guiding Principles, this duty applies to controlled companies as well to all business relationships.
- Civil liability: companies are liable for damage caused by companies under their control. They can discharge this liability if they can prove that they took all due care in line with the HRDD requirement, or that the damage would have occurred even if all due care had been taken.
- Overriding mandatory provision: the aforementioned provisions will apply irrespective of the law applicable under private international law.

The main difference of RBI from Scenario III is that the company's civil liability is not derived from the duty to conduct due diligence, which has a broader scope in RBI. Instead, the company is strictly, vicariously liable for the conduct of controlled entities. This type of liability, which is analogous to liability of employers, parents, or pet owners, provides the company with effective defence of demonstrating due diligence, which is not difficult if the company actually conducted due diligence.

This approach relieves victims of the burden of proving that the company did not exercise due care, evidence of which may not be publicly available. However, they still need to prove damage, illegality, causation between the damage and conduct of the controlled company, and control of the company-defendant over the company causing the damage.

ii) The French duty of vigilance legislative bill The French Parliament is discussing a reform of the Commercial Code recognizing a duty of vigilance of parent companies with content and scope analogous to the concepts outlined in the UN Guiding Principles.

The draft bill, in a version approved by the National Assembly on 23 March 2016,[44] requires large companies[45] to elaborate, effectively implement, and disclose a plan of vigilance. The plan should include appropriate measures to identify and prevent risks of infringements to human rights and fundamental freedoms, risks of serious injuries or environmental harms or health risks, as well as passive or active corruption, resulting directly or indirectly from

44 The draft bill is available at: http://www.assemblee-nationale.fr/14/ta/ta0708.asp, accessed on 30 May 2016. See up to date information on the legislative development on the official French website of legal information: http://www.vie-publique.fr/actualite/panorama/texte-discussion/proposition-loi-relative-au-devoir-vigilance-societes-meres-entreprises-donneuses-ordre.html, accessed 30 May 2016.

45 Those employing more than 5,000 persons in France or above 10,000 employees in France and abroad.

company's activities and activities of companies it controls and of its subcontractors and suppliers, with whom the company has an established business relationship.[46] Details on the content of the plan of vigilance and its implementation are subject to a State Council's decree of application. Every person that has a justifiable interest can require the competent jurisdiction to order a company, subject to penalty, to establish the plan of vigilance, ensure its publication and account for its effective implementation. The bill further provides that non-compliance with this duty gives rise to civil responsibility under French civil code Articles 1382 and 1383, that is, for the damage caused to another by act, imprudence, or negligence.

The duty of vigilance outlined in the bill is similar to Scenario III with several variations. First, it is limited to very large companies. Second, the earlier version of the draft included a rebuttable presumption that linked any damage to a lack or defect of the company's vigilance plan. The current draft leaves the burden of proof on the victim to prove the tort. Third, the specification of control of business partners relies on the definition of an established relationship provided in the legislation. Similarly, the standard of vigilance should be defined in an implementing decree. These definitions may increase legal certainty at the expense, however, of the court's discretion to consider factual control and evolving social expectations concerning the standards of care.

iii) The German civil society proposal A report commissioned by a coalition of NGOs in Germany sets out in detail the case for a duty of care for companies under German law. It proposes the introduction of a statutory duty of care for companies to make a human rights risk analysis, take appropriate preventive measures, and monitor their effectiveness. If a human rights risk has materialized, the company should take measures to attenuate the consequences. In the interest of the (potential) victims, the company must properly document the measures it takes. The statutory duty is both of a public law and a private law nature. First, in the case of a breach of this duty, a public authority can impose a fine on the company. Second, the breach of this duty constitutes the company's liability in tort and entitles the victims of human rights violation to compensation for the damage suffered as a consequence of this violation.[47]

46 These relationships are defined under French law as stable, regular relationships, with or without contract, with a certain volume of business, creating a reasonable expectation that such relation will last. See Code de Commerce, Art L. 442-6-I-5 and the decision of the Cour de Cassation (commercial chamber) of 18 December 2007.

47 R. Klinger *et al.*, *Verankerung menschenrechtlicher Sorgfaltspflichten von Unternehmen im deutschen Recht*, Berlin, Amnesty International *et al.*, 2016. Available at: https://germanwatch.org/de/11970, accessed 30 May 2016.

iv) The United Kingdom Bribery Act The United Kingdom Bribery Act[48] takes a different approach by imposing due diligence as a defence against criminal liability. Section 7(1) of the Bribery Act makes clear that the company's responsibility extends to persons 'associated with the company' if they bribe another person with intention to obtain or retain business or an advantage in the conduct of business for the company. A person associated with the company is defined in section 8 as a person who performs services for or on behalf of the company, for example, as employees, agents, and subsidiaries.

On the other hand, the Bribery Act requires a company only to have procedures in place designed to prevent such persons from committing bribery (section 7(2)). HRDD goes further by focusing on the factual measures taken by the company to prevent, mitigate or cease human rights abuses in which the company is involved and to provide a remedy to victims in case no sufficient and adequate measures were taken.

4.3.3.3 Feasibility

Like Scenario II, this scenario faces the applicable law problem: according to the EU Rome II Regulation,[49] the court must apply the law of the place where the harm occurred. Also here, exceptions may be applicable, but it is not beyond dispute whether they fit this scenario. This issue needs to be clarified by drafting the reform as an overriding mandatory provision in the sense of Article 16 (see above under Scenario II), which would allow the court to apply the law of the forum country, which will usually be the country where the company-defendant is based.

Apart from this obstacle of private international law, this scenario follows the general tendency in the discourse on business and human rights. It expands the boundaries of tort law by requiring companies to look beyond their current legal borders. This seems to be a big step but in practice a large number of companies have already pledged to adhere to the UN Guiding Principles and to implement human rights due diligence. The duty also corresponds with the increasing level of self-regulation in different areas and industries. This implies that many companies follow the principles of corporate responsibility to respect human rights, as expressed in the UN Guiding Principles.

A statutory obligation to conduct due diligence is not necessarily disadvantageous for companies, as there is an increasing need for a level playing field and legal certainty. A company that actually manages its risks properly will carry out due diligence to detect risks in order to minimize any negative impact for the company. In this sense, carrying out due diligence is primarily a risk management tool and not a legal obligation. At the same time, this model encourages

48 Bribery Act 2010 (cl. 23)

49 EU Regulation (EC) No 864/2007 of 11 July 2007 on the law applicable to non-contractual obligations (Rome II), *OJ L-199/40*.

companies to work closely with and to monitor subsidiaries and other business partners to prevent their involvement in human rights abuses, and, where the abuses occur, to mitigate them and provide a remedy at the operational level. Responsibly acting companies that invest means, time, and money in properly carrying out due diligence may be unjustifiably disadvantaged in comparison with companies that do not make these efforts. A statutory duty to carry out HRDD could, therefore, also make a significant contribution towards a level playing field on the EU internal market.

Conclusion

Juan José Álvarez Rubio and Katerina Yiannibas

The challenge as stated above is to adapt to the globalized economy with scrupulous respect for human rights. A new and emerging globalized reality has resulted in an age of radical transformation of our frames of reference. States do not have the capacity to unilaterally address all the problems of this complex world and cannot solve all the needs of its inhabitants. Further multilateral and multilevel governance is required.

On 25 March 1957 the European Economic Community was established at the initiative of the six founding states. Beyond an economic project, it was conceived as a project of peace and freedom at the end of World War II, which had ravaged the European continent. After more than half a century of multilateral cooperation, the utopic dream of peace on the continent has materialized. From its post-war inception, European integration has been based on the protection and promotion of human rights and respect for the rule of law. These must continue to be the basis for any action of the European Union. The recent economic and financial crisis has fatigued and even undermined the engine of European solidarity. It is increasingly tempting (and dangerous for our collective future) to think of every man for himself, to return to protectionism, autarchy. More than ever, the values and principles upon which the EU was built should be considered carefully and upheld respectfully.

The EU defends the universality and indivisibility of human rights through close and active cooperation with third states, international, and regional organizations, as well as associations and groups at all levels of society. Human rights are at the centre of EU relations with other states and regions. With its human rights policy, the EU promotes the rights of women, children, minorities and displaced persons, opposes the death penalty, torture, human trafficking, and discrimination, and defends civil, political, economic, social, and cultural rights. The values of human dignity, freedom, democracy, equality, the rule of law, and respect for human rights are enshrined in the EU treaties. The Charter of Fundamental Rights of the EU is a clear and firm declaration of the rights of EU citizens and establishes that fundamental rights are binding on EU institutions and on Member State governments when they are implementing EU legislation.

In particular, Article 47 of the Charter of Fundamental Rights of the EU reaffirms the EU commitment to respect human rights internationally and enshrines the right to an effective remedy and judicial protection. The task before the European legislator is to promote and ensure effective and efficient access to justice, to further develop a justice system of social protection. This book identifies some solutions to the complex legal and practical challenges associated with access to remedy in order to assist the efforts of the EU and EU Member States to implement the UN Guiding Principles. To this end, the following recommendations are advanced:

a) As concerning the jurisdictional issues for access to judicial remedies

- When deciding on their jurisdiction in private litigation for human rights abuses by multinational companies, state courts of EU Member States must have due regard to their human rights obligations to ensure effective civil remedies under the European Convention on Human Rights and international human rights law.
- EU Member States should consider allowing their domestic courts to exercise jurisdiction over civil claims concerning business-related human rights abuses against subsidiaries, wherever they are based, of companies domiciled within their jurisdiction if such claims are closely connected with civil claims against the latter companies.
- EU Member States' courts should reverse the foreseeability test applied in the ECJ's *Painer* case for joining actions on different legal bases, in cases where parents and subsidiaries are joined together. This would put the burden on the defendant company to prove that it was unforeseeable that the parent may be held jointly liable with the subsidiary, rather than the plaintiffs having to argue that it was foreseeable.
- Where companies are not domiciled within their jurisdiction, EU Member States should consider, or not retreat from, the possibility of allowing their domestic courts to exercise jurisdiction over civil claims concerning business-related human rights abuses against such a business enterprise, if no other effective forum guaranteeing a fair trial is available (*forum necessitatis*), and there is a sufficiently close connection to the Member State concerned.
- EU Member States should consider introducing a rebuttable presumption of control in determining a subsidiary's central administration; a wholly owned or majority-owned subsidiary is presumed to have its central administration with the parent company, unless the parent can prove that the subsidiary makes relevant business decisions independently from the parent and has no ties with the parent's place of incorporation.

b) As concerning the issue of applicable law

- Future case law by the ECJ and the Member State courts on the application of the Rome II Regulation's special rule on environmental damage in civil liability cases involving people and planet-related harm in non-EU host states as a result of the operations of EU-based internationally operating business enterprises should be closely monitored.

- Future case law by the ECJ and the Member State courts on the application of the Rome II Regulation's exceptions on overriding mandatory provisions and public policy and the provision on rules of safety and conduct in civil liability cases involving people and planet-related harm in non-EU host states as a result of the operations of EU-based internationally operating business enterprises should be closely monitored.
- Where necessary, action should be taken at the EU level and/or at the level of the individual Member States to prevent the application of these provisions from hampering the realization of EU (Member States') policies on international corporate social responsibility and business respect for human rights.
- The possibility of extending the scope of the Rome II Regulation's special rule on environmental damage to human rights related damage as well as, possibly, health and safety related damage should be seriously considered.
- Further research should be conducted into the ways in which such an extension could be formulated so as to promote the realization of EU (Member States') policies on international corporate social responsibility and business respect for human rights.

c) As concerning the issue of procedural rules and practical circumstances

- Civil liability cases before EU Member State courts involving people and planet-related harm in non-EU host states as a result of the operations of EU-based internationally operating business enterprises, should be closely monitored so as to identify any procedural rules or practical circumstances that may lead to a denial of justice for victims of corporate human rights or environmental abuse, regardless of the merits of the claim.
- In doing so, the absence of new or further claims in one or more of the Member States, at a time when the prevalence of this type of litigation is strongly on the increase, will be interpreted as an indication that procedural and practical barriers exist in those Member States that render the pursuit of such claims impossible altogether.
- Where necessary, action should be taken by the individual Member States as well as at the EU-level to prevent procedural rules and practical circumstances, especially those relating to costs, collective redress and access to evidence, from resulting in a denial of justice for victims of corporate human rights or environmental abuse.

d) As concerning non-judicial remedies

- Further research is needed (e.g. by academia, civil society)
  - Concerning the experience of individuals and communities that have utilised company-based grievance mechanisms. Based on this, develop for which types of adverse human rights impacts company-based

  - grievance mechanisms are suitable and how they can supplement judicial proceedings.
  - Concerning the effectiveness and follow-up of company-based grievance mechanisms in order to be able to assess whether the mechanisms lead to fair remediation.
- Further guidance from the UN system is needed
  - To develop more specific guidance for the implementation of the UN Guiding Principles in order to ensure effective and rights-based mechanisms, including monitoring of the implementation of company-based grievance mechanisms.
  - To further develop the UN Global Compact's disclosure procedures (Communications on Progress) strengthening the implementation of fully-fledged operational-level grievance mechanisms.
- Action by the EU and its Member States is needed
  - To provide clear guidance for company-based grievance mechanisms e.g. in the EU or National Action Plans on Business and Human Rights, taking into account research on 'good practices' and shortcomings.
  - EU Member States should give a mandate to the PCA to adopt a set of arbitration rules in disputes relating to corporate related human rights abuses. Such rules should provide for transparency, *amicus curiae* participation, collective redress, site visits, specialized arbitrators, financial assistance, and oversight of the implementation of the award.
  - EU Member States should give a mandate to the PCA to adapt the Financial Assistance Fund to provide financial assistance to non-state parties when the subject matter of the dispute involves corporate related human rights abuses.
- Further development at the company level is needed
  - To establish independent entry channels for filing complaints that are dealt with by (ideally, external) stakeholders who strive to achieve equitable solutions for all parties.
  - To strengthen trust in the procedures by ensuring confidentiality of individual complaints handled by external stakeholders.
  - To provide more information to (potential) victims of corporate related human rights abuse so that they have adequate knowledge about channels available to obtain redress and can choose the best option according to their specific situations. Ensure that the information is delivered in a culturally and linguistically appropriate way and takes into account fear of reprisals.

As concerning corporate responsibility vis-à-vis a legal duty of care, three complimentary options for legal reform are proposed:

- Scenario I: facilitating victims' access to evidence of the defendant-company's control over its business partner, e.g. subsidiary or contractor, that has committed the alleged human rights abuses.

- Scenario II: in terms of burden of proof, presuming the existence of such control when certain conditions are met that show control, prima facie.
- Scenario III: introducing a company's statutory duty to identify, prevent and take action to cease human rights abuses by its business partners, analogous to the human rights due diligence outlined in the UN Guiding Principles.

The EU has an opportunity to lead by example, to adopt legal instruments that demonstrate that it is possible to promote international trade and the protection of human rights both within and outside the EU. Law is a tool for achieving this objective strategically. The technical dimension of legal reform is the work of research and, in this case, the result of an academic alliance of legal scholars and practitioners with the support of the European Commission. At the dawn of the twenty-first century, Europe faces one of the most important challenges in its history: to build a new model of political coexistence, a new form of democracy that, beyond the mere juxtaposition of current political systems, is capable of global leadership in social justice and sustainable development. Europe must respond to the challenges of the twenty-first century courageously and innovatively. In these uncertain times, the EU is in a unique position to promote a model for social and political organization based not on interest but, above all, on values.

Index

For Product Safety Concerns and Information please contact our EU representative GPSR@taylorandfrancis.com
Taylor & Francis Verlag GmbH, Kaufingerstraße 24, 80331 München, Germany

www.ingramcontent.com/pod-product-compliance
Ingram Content Group UK Ltd.
Pitfield, Milton Keynes, MK11 3LW, UK
UKHW022123190926
475702UK00013B/1604
9780367025168